Discover
Britain's
historic
houses

London
Berkshire & Surrey

Discover Britain's

Published by Reader's Digest Association Ltd
London • New York • Sydney • Montreal

historic houses

London
Berkshire & Surrey

Simon Jenkins

Contents

4 LONDON WEST

1 BERKSHIRE

5 SURREY

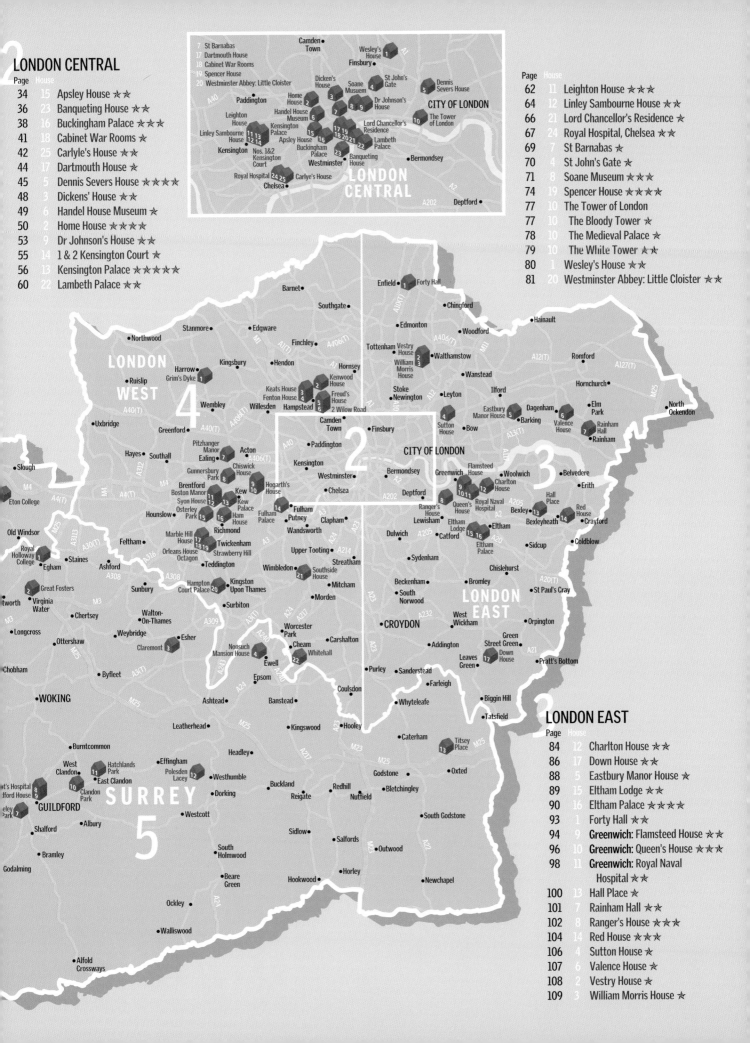

LONDON CENTRAL

LONDON EAST

The best in Britain

SCOTLAND

- 114 Abbotsford, Melrose
- 127 Blair Castle
- 130 Cawdor Castle
- 128 Craigievar Castle
- 112 Drumlanrig Castle
- 131 Dunrobin Castle
- 129 Dunvegan Castle

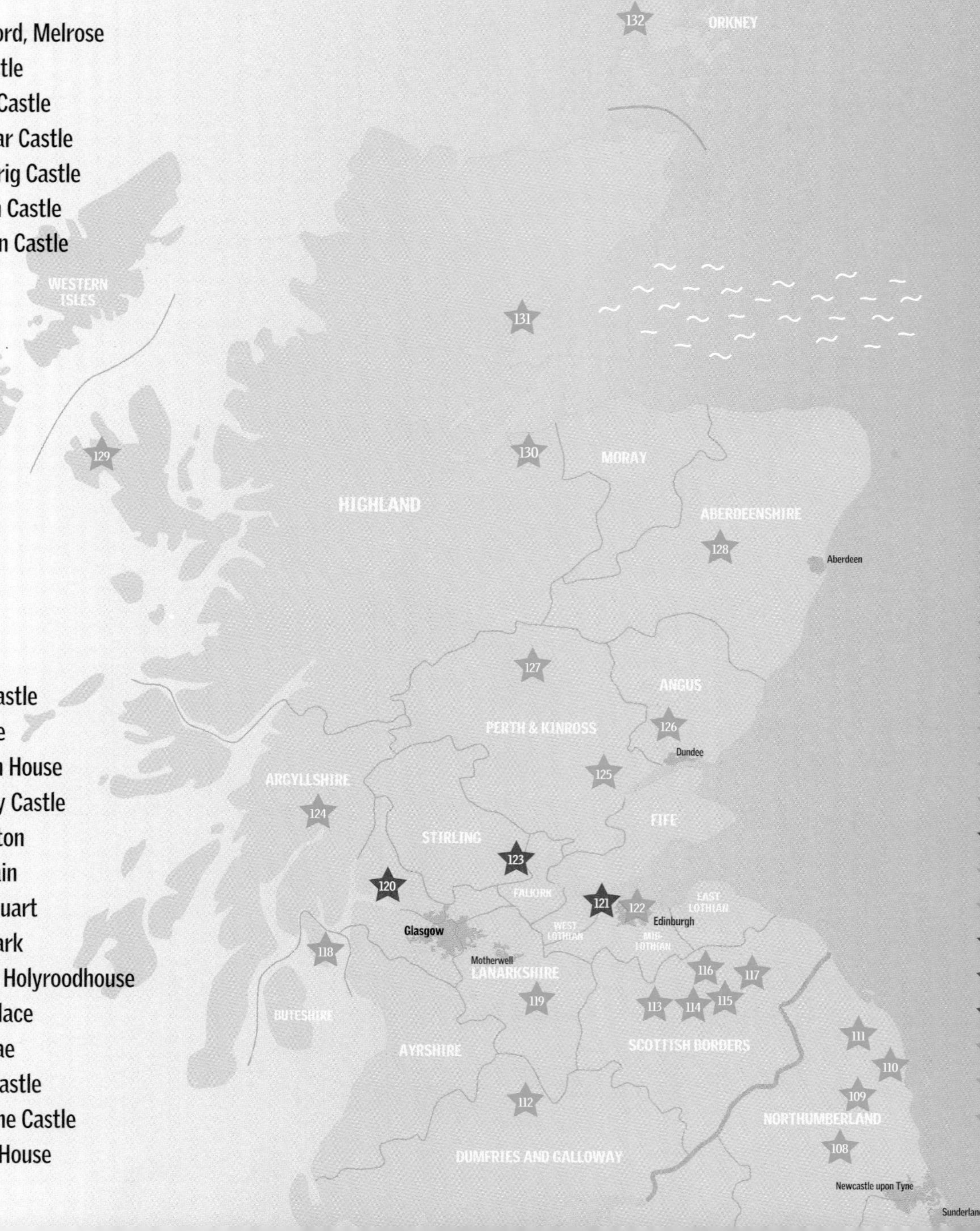

ORKNEY
132
WESTERN ISLES
131
129
130
MORAY
HIGHLAND
ABERDEENSHIRE
128
Aberdeen
127
ANGUS
PERTH & KINROSS
126
Dundee
125
ARGYLLSHIRE
124
FIFE
STIRLING
123
120
FALKIRK
121
122
EAST LOTHIAN
Edinburgh
WEST LOTHIAN
MID-LOTHIAN
Glasgow
118
Motherwell
LANARKSHIRE
116
117
119
113
114
115
BUTESHIRE
AYRSHIRE
SCOTTISH BORDERS
111
110
109
112
NORTHUMBERLAND
108
DUMFRIES AND GALLOWAY
Newcastle upon Tyne
Sunderland

- 126 Glamis Castle
- 120 Hill House
- 121 Hopetoun House
- 124 Inveraray Castle
- 117 Manderston
- 115 Mellerstain
- 118 Mount Stuart
- 119 New Lanark
- 122 Palace of Holyroodhouse
- 125 Scone Palace
- 132 Skara Brae
- 123 Stirling Castle
- 116 Thirlestane Castle
- 113 Traquair House

- 61 Canons Ashby
- 102 Castle Howard
- 14 Charleston
- 54 Chastleton
- 91 Chatsworth House
- 111 Chillingham Castle
- 36 Chiswick House *
- 56 Claydon House
- 16 Cothay Manor
- 109 Cragside
- 70 Deene Park
- 38 Dennis Severs House *
- 28 Dyrham Park
- 52 Eastnor Castle
- 40 Eltham Palace *
- 100 Fairfax House
- 13 Firle Place
- 3 Forde Abbey
- 27 Godinton Park
- 8 Goodwood House
- 78 Grimsthorpe Castle
- 90 Haddon Hall
- 66 Hagley Hall
- 35 Ham House *
- 34 Hampton Court *
- 93 Hardwick Hall
- 98 Harewood House
- 76 Harlaxton Manor
- 65 Harvington Hall
- 51 Hatfield House
- 22 Hever Castle
- 80 Holkham Hall
- 37 Home House *
- 79 Houghton Hall
- 107 Hutton-in-the-Forest
- 25 Ightham Mote
- 74 Kedleston Hall
- 21 Kensington Palace *
- 5 Kingston Lacy
- 50 Knebworth House
- 24 Knole
- 29 Lacock Abbey
- 1 Lanhydrock
- 26 Leeds Castle
- 104 Levens Hall
- 19 Longleat
- 89 Lyme Park
- 53 Madresfield Court
- 48 Magdalen College
- 17 Montacute House
- 101 Newby Hall
- 94 Newstead Abbey
- 96 Nostell Priory
- 6 Osborne House
- 32 Osterley Park *
- 72 Oxburgh Hall
- 10 Parham House
- 23 Penshurst Place
- 9 Petworth House
- 106 Raby Castle
- 59 Ragley Hall
- 41 Restoration House

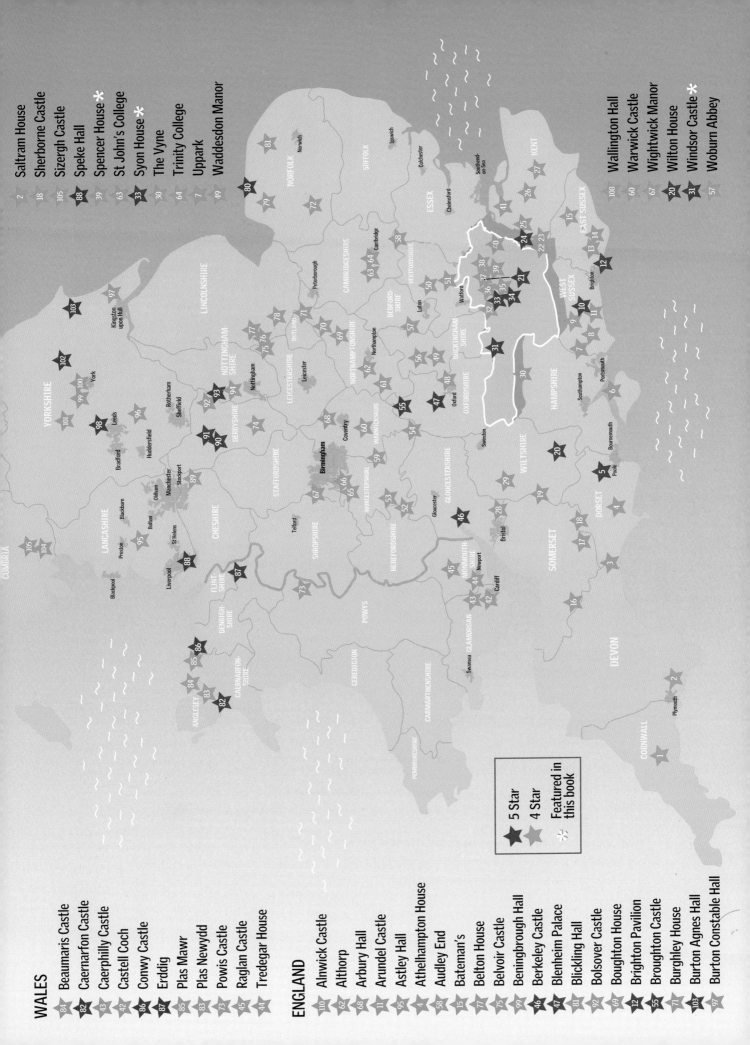

WALES

84	Beaumaris Castle	
82	Caernarfon Castle	⭐
43	Caerphilly Castle	
42	Castell Coch	
86	Conwy Castle	⭐
87	Erddig	
85	Plas Mawr	
83	Plas Newydd	
73	Powis Castle	
45	Raglan Castle	
44	Tredegar House	

ENGLAND

110	Alnwick Castle	
62	Althorp	
68	Arbury Hall	
11	Arundel Castle	
95	Astley Hall	
4	Athelhampton House	
58	Audley End	
15	Bateman's	
77	Belton House	
75	Belvoir Castle	
99	Beningbrough Hall	
46	Berkeley Castle	⭐
47	Blenheim Palace	⭐
81	Blickling Hall	
92	Bolsover Castle	
69	Boughton House	
12	Brighton Pavilion	⭐
55	Broughton Castle	⭐
71	Burghley House	
103	Burton Agnes Hall	⭐
97	Burton Constable Hall	

2	Saltram House	
18	Sherborne Castle	
105	Sizergh Castle	
88	Speke Hall	⭐
39	Spencer House	✳
63	St John's College	
33	Syon House	✳
30	The Vyne	
64	Trinity College	
7	Uppark	
49	Waddesdon Manor	

108	Wallington Hall	
60	Warwick Castle	
67	Wightwick Manor	
20	Wilton House	⭐
31	Windsor Castle	✳
57	Woburn Abbey	

KEY

⭐ 5 Star
⭐ 4 Star
✳ Featured in this book

I visited these buildings after writing a book on English churches and the experience was as moving as it was different. While places of worship were built according to the authority and liturgy of the Church, people built houses for themselves. A house was useful first and beautiful second, and from this derives the joy of visiting houses. They are a conversation between utility and beauty down the ages.

In defining the word 'house' I soon found that I could not sensibly distinguish castle from palace, house from hut, roof from ruin. My list embraces any structure in which men and women have laid their heads, provided that they are in some degree accessible to public view. The selection is a personal list and the commentary is a personal vision, warts and all.

Simon Jenkins

Historic houses
of London, Berkshire & Surrey

The Royal County of **Berkshire** guards the southern bank of the Thames and embraces Slough, Windsor, Maidenhead and Reading. Its royalty is based on its one great building, Windsor Castle, so little visited by the English yet the most palatial house in England. Although a castle since Norman times, it is principally a monument to Restoration taste and 19th-century neo-Gothic splendour. It is also one of England's finest art galleries. In Windsor's shadow is the old school of Eton, built round a medieval core. At Basildon is Carr of York's only southern house, saved by the Iliffe family. The home of Elizabeth's trusted Walsingham is at Englefield. Bear Wood is a colossal Victorian fantasmagoria.

The houses of **Central London** were first dominated by the palaces of the Crown, then of the aristocracy, then of the plutocracy. Only later do we encounter town houses of the middle class, accessible usually because of a famous resident. The City of London has no domestic houses open, but on its border is the medieval enclave of the Tower, with the remains of a castle, royal palace and early street. Medieval work also survives in the hinterland of the abbey at Westminster and as part of Lambeth Palace.

West of the City, a fragment of Whitehall Palace survives in Inigo Jones's Banqueting House. Nash's Buckingham Palace and Wren's Kensington Palace – an under-appreciated gem – are both now accessible. Spencer House and Apsley House are two of the few large aristocratic West End palaces to have survived. On a smaller scale is the eccentric residence built by Sir John Soane in Lincoln's Inn Fields. A selection of 18th-century town houses includes those of John Wesley, Dr Johnson, Dickens, Handel and Carlyle. The most successful domestic re-creation is the Dennis Severs House in Spitalfields. The residences of Lord Leighton and Linley Sambourne are memorials to two Victorian artists.

Downstream is the business end of any maritime city and the suburbs of **East London** have always been the poor relation. The best land was in Greenwich, Eltham and Woodford, and it is here that we find the finest houses. The most notable group, overlooking the Thames at Greenwich, is one of the best architectural set pieces in England: James I's Queen's House, Charles II's Greenwich Palace (later the Royal Naval Hospital) and, on the hill behind, Wren's observatory, Flamsteed House.

Otherwise, the better houses were built in what was then countryside, in adjacent Essex and Kent. Eastbury Manor House and Hall Place are Elizabethan. Charlton House is, or could be, one of the best Jacobean houses in the capital. Rainham Hall is a beacon of civility on the Essex marshes, while Eltham Palace has England's best surviving Art Deco interiors.

As London spread steadily west across the Middlesex plain, some of the finest domestic architecture in England arose in **West London**. Wolsey and Henry VIII led the way, together creating the great palace at Hampton Court. Wealth soon followed: the Greshams rebuilt Osterley, the Percys took on Syon. In the 17th century Dutch classicism came to Kew Palace, while the Restoration turned Hampton Court into one of the most entrancing palaces in Europe. The Georgian colonization of Richmond brought a brief Augustan Elysium to the Thames bank. George II's mistress, Lady Suffolk, built Marble Hill. Horace Walpole created his Gothick import at Strawberry Hill. Then, in the 1760s, Robert Adam arrived to give Syon and Osterley some of his finest interiors.

The north-western heights of the capital saw more modest colonization. Adam's house at Kenwood is one of his lesser works. Across the Heath is Keats' Hampstead villa and the Victorian property acquired by Sigmund Freud on his escape from Vienna. A Modern Movement icon can be seen in Willow Road.

Today, the North Downs of **Surrey** are the county's one haven of calm. Until the coming of the railway, they were a barrier to development south from London. There were few big estates, only thick beech, oak and chestnut woods. The Bishops of Winchester built Farnham Castle, with keep, tower and fine interiors. Loseley is a substantial Elizabethan mansion, believed to contain woodwork from vanished Nonsuch. The county also has a Palladian epic at Clandon. Of a later date is Mrs Greville's treasure trove of art at Polesden Lacey, while a similar collector's house survives at picturesque Titsey. Connoisseurs of eccentric Victoriana cannot miss the Royal Holloway College above Egham.

✫ STAR RATINGS AND ACCESSIBILITY ✫✫✫✫✫

The 'star' ratings are entirely my personal choice (but see note below). They rate the overall quality of the house as presented to the public, and not gardens or other attractions. On balance I scaled down houses, however famous, for not being easily accessible or for being only partly open.

The top rating, five stars, is given to those houses that qualify as 'international' celebrities. Four stars are awarded to houses of outstanding architectural quality and public display. Three-star houses comprise the run of good historic houses, well displayed and worthy of national promotion. Two and one-star houses are of more local interest, are hard to visit, or have just one significant feature.

Accessibility varies greatly, from buildings that are open all year to houses that can only be visited 'by appointment' (rarely, I have broken my rule and included a private property that is not open at all, but is viewable from nearby walks or public gardens). Opening hours tend to alter from year to year, but an indication of how accessible a house is to visitors is given at the start of each entry, together with brief information on location and ownership. Many of the houses are National Trust or English Heritage properties, some are now museums or hotels, others are privately owned by families who open to the public for part of the year (English Heritage grant requirements insist on 28 days minimum). Some owners may, understandably, seek to cluster visitors on particular days. More details for each house are given at the back of this book, and readers are advised to check before visiting.

A final note, houses are, or should be, living things subject to constant change and how we view them is bound to be a subject of debate. I welcome any correction or comment, especially from house owners, sent to me c/o the publisher.

NOTE: On the UK map (pages 6-7) the 4 and 5-star houses in England and Wales were selected by Simon Jenkins. Those in Scotland were selected by Hamish Scott and the editors of Reader's Digest.

Architectural timeline
and houses in brief

Apsley House
The Duke of Wellington's London home from 1817. Built in 1771 by Robert Adam, and embellished by Benjamin Dean Wyatt.

Banqueting House
Remnant of the royal palace of Whitehall. Designed by Inigo Jones on Palladian lines in 1619, with ceiling by Peter Paul Rubens.

Basildon Park
The only southern house designed by John Carr of York, rescued in the 1950s. The interiors reflect the influence of Robert Adam.

Bear Wood
A massive Victorian mansion, inspired by Elizabethan architecture but built with all mod cons of the 19th century.

Boston Manor
Red-brick Jacobean manor built in 1623, updated in the 1670s probably under the influence of Inigo Jones.

Buckingham Palace
Royal palace built around an early 18th-century building by John Nash for George IV. Side wings are Victorian, by Edward Blore; the façade, by Sir Aston Webb, dates to 1913.

Cabinet War Rooms
Basement in Whitehall, converted to Churchill's command centre in WWII.

Carlyle's House
Queen-Anne terraced house in Chelsea, home of Thomas and Jane Carlyle from 1834. Preserved as a typical middle-class Victorian home.

Charlton House
Jacobean E-plan house, c1607–12, with Mannerist Renaissance frontispiece. Original ceilings, fireplaces and staircases survive.

Chiswick: Chiswick House
Built by Lord Burlington, c1725, as a garden pavilion. Burlington was one of the founders of the 18th-century Palladian revival. The interiors are by William Kent.

Chiswick: Hogarth's House
Red-brick house, built c1700. The artist and satirist William Hogarth lived here from 1749 until his death in 1764. Some restored Georgian panelling survives.

Clandon Park
Palladian mansion built by the Venetian architect, Giacomo Leoni. The two-storey Marble Hall features a magnificent stucco ceiling.

Claremont
Vanbrugh house remodelled for Clive of India by Capability Brown and Brown's son-in-law, Henry Holland.

Dartmouth House
Banker's Mayfair town house, rebuilt in 1890 in French style, with suitably grand entrance.

Dennis Severs House
A simple 18th-century town house near Spitalfields, once the home of silk weavers, transformed inside by an American collector.

Dickens' House
Early 19th-century house in Doughty Street, home to Charles Dickens in the early years of his marriage, now a museum.

Down House
Charles Darwin's country home from 1842, where he wrote *On the Origin of Species*. The ground floor has been restored as it would have been during Darwin's occupation.

Eastbury Manor House
Tudor mansion, built in brick. The Great Hall and Great Chamber above have survived, the latter with some fine wall paintings.

Eltham Lodge
Restoration mansion by architect Hugh May, showing the influence of Dutch architecture. An original staircase and features survive.

Eltham Palace
The remains of a medieval palace, extended in the 1930s. The Art-Deco interiors are among the finest in England.

Englefield House
Elizabethan mansion, the exterior much remodelled by the Victorians and with rooms redecorated in 18th, 19th and 20th centuries. The original Long Gallery has been restored.

Eton College
A set of historic buildings grouped around courtyards. The earliest ranges date back to the late 15th century, but important structures were added in the 17th and 18th centuries.

Farnham Castle
Castle of the Bishops of Winchester with 12th-century keep, bailey and curtain wall. The bishop's residence, which includes a Great Hall and Tudor rooms, was rebuilt after the Civil War.

Fenton House
William-and-Mary house built around 1693 and little changed over the years. A balcony at roof level is a particular feature.

Forty Hall
Early 17th-century house with rare classical façade, possibly influenced by Inigo Jones. An 18th-century entrance hall has fine plasterwork.

Freud's House
Red-brick Hampstead house, built in Queen-Anne style in the inter-war years and Freud's home after fleeing the Nazis. His famous study is preserved.

Fulham Palace
Country palace of the Bishops of London, established in the 12th century. Now made up of two buildings, one Tudor and one mid-Georgian, arranged round two courtyards.

Godalming: Red House
Early work by Edwin Lutyens, built in red-brick on a steep slope and overlooking a valley. The gardens were by Gertrude Jekyll.

Great Fosters
Tudor house with surviving Jacobean details inside, given a country-house makeover in the early 20th century.

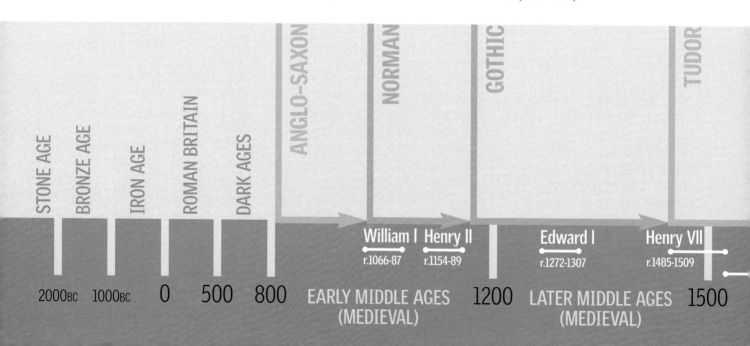

STONE AGE • BRONZE AGE • IRON AGE • ROMAN BRITAIN • DARK AGES • ANGLO-SAXON • NORMAN • GOTHIC • TUDOR

William I r.1066-87 | Henry II r.1154-89 | Edward I r.1272-1307 | Henry VII r.1485-1509

2000BC | 1000BC | 0 | 500 | 800 | EARLY MIDDLE AGES (MEDIEVAL) | 1200 | LATER MIDDLE AGES (MEDIEVAL) | 1500

Greenwich: Flamsteed House
House built by Wren, c1676, for John Flamsteed, Astronomer Royal. The Octagon Room was Flamsteed's observatory.

Greenwich: Queen's House
Inigo Jones's innovative house for James I's wife, the first Palladian building in England, begun in 1616. Work halted with her death in 1619 and only resumed in 1629.

Greenwich: Royal Naval Hospital
Begun by John Webb as a palace for Charles II, became a naval hospital under William and Mary with the addition of a Hawksmoor wing. Finished by Wren as English Baroque.

Grim's Dyke
Neo-Tudor country house, designed in the 1870s by Norman Shaw for the artist Frederick Goodall. Bought in 1890 by W. S. Gilbert and altered by the firm of Ernest George & Peto.

Guildford: Abbot's Hospital
An almshouse founded in 1619 by George Abbot. The Hospital is entered through a Jacobean gatehouse; its buildings are ranged around a quadrangle.

Guildford: Guildford House
A 17th-century town house, the façade dominated by its windows and divided by four classical pilasters. A 17th-century balcony survives over the front door.

Gunnersbury Park
Early 18th-century mansion, once owned by the Rothschilds who commissioned Sydney Smirke to add new reception rooms and an Orangery.

Hall Place
A 16th-century hall house, with Great Hall and wings, in stone and flint. A red-brick Restoration courtyard was added in the 17th century.

Ham House
Jacobean house given classical embellishments in the 1670s, when a set of state rooms were also created on the first floor; the family rooms were at ground level.

Hampton Court Palace
Tudor riverside palace of Cardinal Wolsey, seized and then embellished by Henry VIII. William and Mary added a grand complex of twin state rooms in the 17th century.

Palladianism

The style known as Palladianism was inspired by the Italian architect, Andrea Palladio (1508–80). His most influential buildings were the palazzos and villas that he designed and built in and around Vicenza. These elegant structures adhered to strict rules of proportion and symmetry that Palladio had derived by studying the architecture of ancient Rome. His writings on architecture, in particular his *Quattro libri dell architettura* (1570), had a profound effect.

In the 17th century, Inigo Jones first introduced Palladian principles to English architecture in the Queen's House, Greenwich (see page 96), but it was the 18th century that saw the main use of the style in Britain in a period of Palladian revival. In the words of Nikolaus Pevsner: '[Palladio] appealed to the civilized taste and the polite learning of the Georgian gentry more than any other architect.' Colen Campbell was the first architect of the revival; his Wanstead House (1715, now demolished) became the model for the Palladian country house and won him the patronage of Lord Burlington, the 'architect Earl'.

Influenced by Campbell and by the publication of the first English edition of Palladio's *Quattro libri*, Burlington took up the style for his own work and designed several Palladian buildings himself. His most important surviving work is Chiswick House in West London (c1725, see page 113), based on Palladio's Villa Rotunda (c1550–4) in Vicenza. Burlington and his protegé William Kent went on to dominate British architecture for several decades, making Palladianism a highly fashionable style for country houses built in Britain in the 18th century.

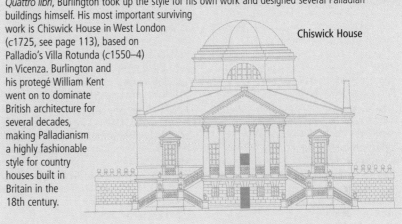

Chiswick House

Handel House Museum
Handel moved into his home in Brook Street in 1723, soon after the house was built as part of the Georgian development of London.

Hatchlands Park
Begun in the 1750s, the house has an exterior is by Stiff Leadbetter, interiors by Robert Adam, and a park by Humphry Repton. Today, it houses the Cobbe Collection.

Home House
Robert Adam's London masterpiece, a Georgian town house on a grand scale. Now a private London club, the interiors have been restored to their former grandeur.

Dr Johnson's House
William-and-Mary town house in the City, home of Dr Johnson from 1748 to 1759. The garret studio was where his Dictionary was compiled.

Keats House
The Regency house, built by Keats's friend Charles Brown, that the poet moved to in 1818. The rooms he occupied are preserved much as he left them.

Nos. 1 & 2 Kensington Court
Two late Victorian town houses: No.1, by J. J. Stevenson, has Dutch gables and a corner turret; No.2 was built in a Franco-Flemish Gothic style by T. G. Jackson.

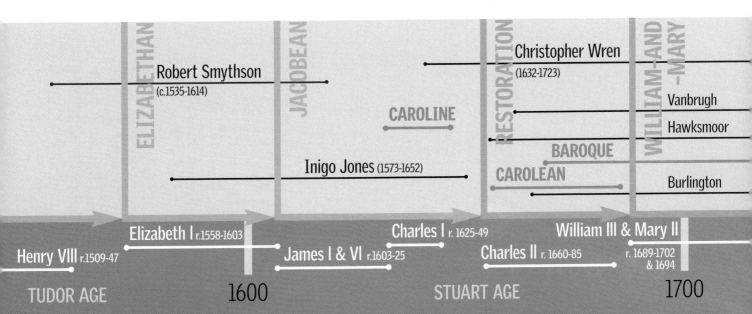

ELIZABETHAN — JACOBEAN — CAROLINE — RESTORATION — WILLIAM-AND-MARY

Robert Smythson (c.1535-1614)

Inigo Jones (1573-1652)

Christopher Wren (1632-1723)

CAROLEAN — BAROQUE

Vanbrugh

Hawksmoor

Burlington

Henry VIII r.1509-47

Elizabeth I r.1558-1603

James I & VI r.1603-25

Charles I r. 1625-49

Charles II r. 1660-85

William III & Mary II r. 1689-1702 & 1694

TUDOR AGE — 1600 — STUART AGE — 1700

Inigo Jones (1573–1652)

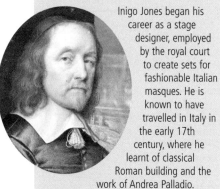

Inigo Jones began his career as a stage designer, employed by the royal court to create sets for fashionable Italian masques. He is known to have travelled in Italy in the early 17th century, where he learnt of classical Roman building and the work of Andrea Palladio.

In 1615, Jones became Surveyor of the King's Works, a post he occupied until 1642. His first work for James I was the Queen's House in Greenwich (begun 1616, see page 96). This was the first house in England built on Palladian lines, and it was radically different from anything before. The departure from Jacobean style is immediately obvious in a comparison of the Queen's House with any near-contemporary structure, such as Charlton House (see page 84). Comparison with Marble Hill House (see page 142), built more than a century later, shows Jones to be the forefather of 18th-century Palladianism.

For his next major building, the Banqueting House (see page 36), Jones employed the radical concept of basing its proportions on a double cube. Between 1625 and 1640 he worked on two main projects: Covent Garden, which he based on an Italian piazza, and the remodelling of the medieval St Paul's Cathedral.

At the start of the Civil War in 1642, Jones's property was seized. Little is then known of him for several years, but he was pardoned in 1646 and his estate returned. It is believed that he advised his nephew John Webb on the design of Wilton House, in Wiltshire, during his last years.

Kensington Palace
Originally Jacobean, the house was extended into a palace for William and Mary by Wren and Hawksmoor. George I had further alterations made by Colen Campbell and William Kent.

Kenwood House
Mansion house high on Hampstead Heath, remodelled by Robert Adam in the 1760s. Saved from demolition in the 1920s by Lord Iveagh, and now home to his magnificent art collection.

Kew Palace
Built in 1631 by a London merchant, this Dutch-style brick house was George III's home during his bouts of illness. The early 19th-century interiors have been re-created.

Lambeth Palace
London home of the Archbishops of Canterbury. Much of the medieval palace was replaced by Victorian buildings. The Great Hall dates to the early 17th century.

Leighton House
Red-brick house built by Victorian artist Frederic Leighton in 1864. Inside, the Arab Hall is decorated with Leighton's collection of antique tiles from the Middle East.

Linley Sambourne House
Home of a Victorian artist and photographer, Edward Linley Sambourne. The rooms have been restored to how he left them, full of his and his family's personal effects.

Lord Chancellor's Residence
Apartment within the Palace of Westminster decorated and furnished with reproduction Pugin fixtures and fittings.

Loseley Park
The E-plan house of an Elizabethan courtier. The Great Hall features panelling said to come from Henry VIII's Nonsuch Palace.

Marble Hill House
A Palladian villa on the river Thames, built for George II's 'mistress'. The Great Room rises up through the top two storeys of the house.

Nonsuch Mansion House
A mansion begun in 1802 on the site of an old outbuilding of the demolished Nonsuch Palace. Built in Gothick style by Sir Jeffry Wyatville.

Orleans House Octagon
Originally a pavilion for the garden of James Johnston's Orleans House (now demolished), the Octagon was designed by James Gibb in 1720, in typical early-Georgian style.

Osterley Park
Elizabethan mansion, remodelled in the 17th century by Robert Adam. Adam enclosed the courtyard with a pedimented loggia and transformed the interiors.

Pitzhanger Manor
Sir John Soane demolished all but the Georgian wing of the original Pitzhanger Manor and rebuilt the house, from 1800–10, in a style of his own interpretation of classical architecture.

Polesden Lacey
Neo-classical Regency villa, built among the North Downs by Thomas Cubitt. The interiors were transformed by Edwardian society hostess, Mrs Ronald Greville.

Rainham Hall
Georgian house with remnants of Queen Anne style. The interior retains original panelling and fireplaces; the staircase has trompe-l'œil paintings.

Ranger's House
William-and-Mary house with Georgian wings, overlooking Blackheath. Home to the Wernher collection of art and jewellery.

Red House
William Morris's first family home, designed by Phillip Webb in 1859. A red-brick house, it's an early example of an Arts-and-Crafts building.

Royal Holloway College
A college for young ladies built by the entrepreneur Thomas Holloway and opened in 1886. The architect W. H. Crossland based the building on a Loire chateau.

Royal Hospital Chelsea
A home for retired soldiers designed by Sir Christopher Wren. Begun in 1682, it is set around three courtyards, with classical porticos and an elongated cupola.

St Barnabas
Georgian town house in Soho, built in 1746. Some of the rooms have fine Rococo plasterwork.

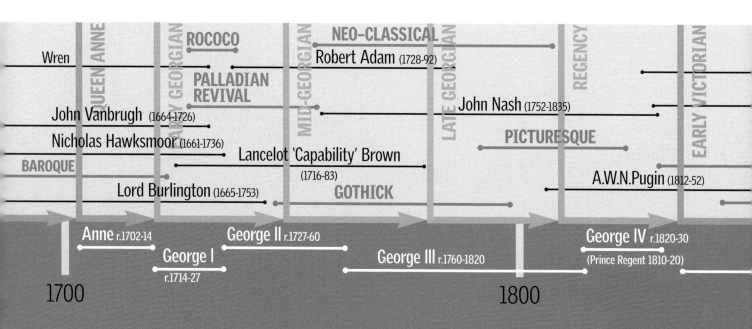

Wren

QUEEN ANNE

EARLY GEORGIAN

ROCOCO

PALLADIAN REVIVAL

NEO-CLASSICAL

Robert Adam (1728–92)

MID-GEORGIAN

LATE GEORGIAN

REGENCY

EARLY VICTORIAN

John Vanbrugh (1664–1726)

Nicholas Hawksmoor (1661–1736)

BAROQUE

Lord Burlington (1665–1753)

Lancelot 'Capability' Brown (1716–83)

GOTHICK

John Nash (1752–1835)

PICTURESQUE

A.W.N.Pugin (1812–52)

1700

Anne r.1702–14

George I r.1714–27

George II r.1727–60

George III r.1760–1820

George IV r.1820–30 (Prince Regent 1810–20)

1800

St John's Gate
Remains of the headquarters of the Knights Hospitallers of St John of Jerusalem, established on the site in 1140.

Soane Museum
Beginning in 1792, architect Sir John Soane rebuilt three houses in Lincoln's Inn Fields as a home for his family and his collection of paintings, sculpture and artefacts.

Southside House
Restoration house, much amended and added to over the centuries and still reflecting the personal taste of its owners in style and decoration.

Spencer House
Palladian mansion in St James's Place, built by John Vardy for the 1st Earl Spencer in the 1750s. The sumptuous interiors are mainly by James 'Athenian' Stuart.

Strawberry Hill
Horace Walpole's Gothick fantasy, begun 1749. The architecture and design of the interiors drew on Romantic interpretations of medieval Gothic style.

Sutton House
A 16th-century mansion built by Sir Richard Sadleir, courtier of Henry VIII. Some 17th-century wall painting survives and original linenfold panelling has been restored.

Syon House
Tudor house transformed inside by Robert Adam in the 1760s. Adam left the exterior unchanged but created some of his greatest rooms within.

Titsey Place
Hidden among the North Downs, a house of Tudor origins, rebuilt in 1775 in the Georgian era, then again in 1826 by William Atkinson in a neo-Tudor style.

Tower of London
The White Tower (c1078) is the largest and best-preserved Norman keep in England. The Medieval Palace was built by Henry III and Edward I during the 13th century. The Bloody Tower, built c1225, housed Sir Walter Raleigh during his imprisonment in the early 17th century.

Valence House
A 17th-century house built on the site of a 13th-century manor around the remains of a 15th-century building. Part of the moat survives.

Vestry House
A dark brick house, built in 1730, which has had a variety of uses during its history: once a workhouse, it came to be used by the Metropolitan Police.

Welford Park
Late 17th-century mansion in red brick, probably by John Jackson of Oxford. The interior was refashioned around the stairwell in the 1830s.

Wesley's House
The house was built in 1779 next to the new Methodist Chapel in the City Road. Wesley lived on the first floor while the rest of the house was home to preachers of the London Circuit and their families.

Westminster Abbey: Little Cloister
A group of residential buildings, the remains of the old monastery deep in the heart of the Abbey complex, ranged around a courtyard.

Whitehall
A timber-framed house, begun c1500, covered in white clapboard. The two-storeyed hall was built with a chimney, a modern innovation at the time.

William Morris House
A large Georgian mansion, built in 1762 in once-rural Walthamstow. Home to William Morris from the age of 13.

2 Willow Road
The centre house in row of three, designed by Modernist architect Ernö Goldfinger in 1934. The house, in which Goldfinger himself lived, was highly controversial when first built.

Windsor Castle
Massive royal residence, dominated by the great Norman Round Tower and extended by various monarchs – Edward III, Charles I, George III and George IV – during its long history.

Windsor Castle: Queen Mary's Dolls' House
A perfect royal home in miniature, designed by Sir Edwin Lutyens in his 'Wrenaissance style' and complete with a garden by Gertrude Jekyll.

Sir Christopher Wren (1632–1723)

Early in his career, Wren looked set to become a man of science. Praised by Newton and a founding member of the Royal Society, he was Professor of Astronomy at Oxford by 1661. Architecture was just one branch of science in which he had an interest. His earliest designs – the Sheldonian Theatre, Oxford, and Pembroke College Chapel, Cambridge – have been described as the work of a gifted amateur, showing great skill in structural engineering but less in design. In 1664 he travelled in France and the Low Countries, where he met Bernini, Mansart and Le Vau, and this was to be highly influential on his style.

After the Fire of London (1666), Wren was appointed to the Royal Commission for rebuilding, and by 1669 he was Surveyor General of the King's Works. His overall city plan was rejected, but he rebuilt St Paul's (1675–1709) and 51 churches. St Paul's was his masterpiece, combining classical elements, particularly the dome, with baroque in the towers, façade and interior.

Of his secular buildings, the Royal Naval Hospital in Greenwich is the most baroque (see page 98). His earlier Chelsea Hospital (see page 67) is more restrained and classical in style. He created grand additions to Whitehall and Winchester palaces and to Hampton Court, but of these only a fragment at Hampton survives (see page 130). Wren lost his position as King's Surveyor in 1714, on the accession of George I. He died aged 91, having, he wrote, 'made some figure in the world'.

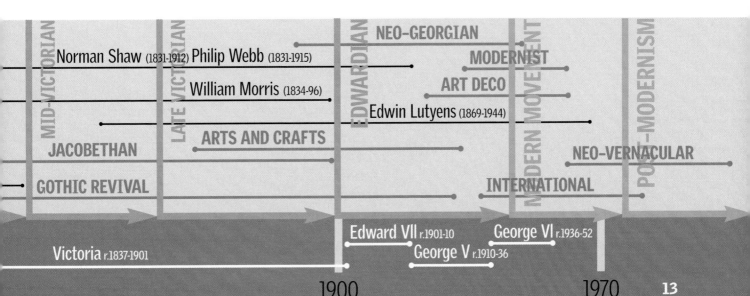

berk

Windsor Castle

shire

Berkshire

Basildon park

★★★ John Carr of York's only house in the south, now a masterpiece of restoration

Near Pangbourne, 7 miles NW of Reading; National Trust, open part year

When Lady Iliffe discovered Basildon Park in 1952 there was 'no window ... left intact, and most were repaired with cardboard or plywood; there was a large puddle on the Library floor'. She found walls still covered in Army graffiti, which the Army felt no obligation to clean when it vacated the house after occupation during the Second World War. All seemed hopeless. Yet the Iliffes cherished this place for twenty-five years and handed it beautifully restored to the National Trust. When I arrived, after trudging from the distant car park through heavy rain, I was rudely ordered to stop writing notes in the guidebook on pain of eviction. Note-taking is not allowed here. Students should stay away for fear of worse.

Basildon as left by the Iliffes is immaculate. It was built in 1776 by John Carr of York, his one building in the south, for the Indian nabob, Sir Francis Sykes. It was then sold in 1838 to a Liberal MP, James Morrison, but after his daughter died in 1910 the contents were sold and the building decayed. Some of its best plasterwork went to the Waldorf Astoria in New York (for its 'Basildon Room'). Not until the Iliffes chanced upon the house after the war did it recover its soul. Basildon is their monument as much as Carr's.

The west façade, in honeyed Bath stone, is a harmonious composition of portico, basement and wings. It might be a town house overlooking Piccadilly. The entrance is hidden behind three arched openings, up stairs from a loggia and behind the portico. Visitors thus half-enter the building, go out onto the portico, then come into the hall through a theatrical sequence of spaces.

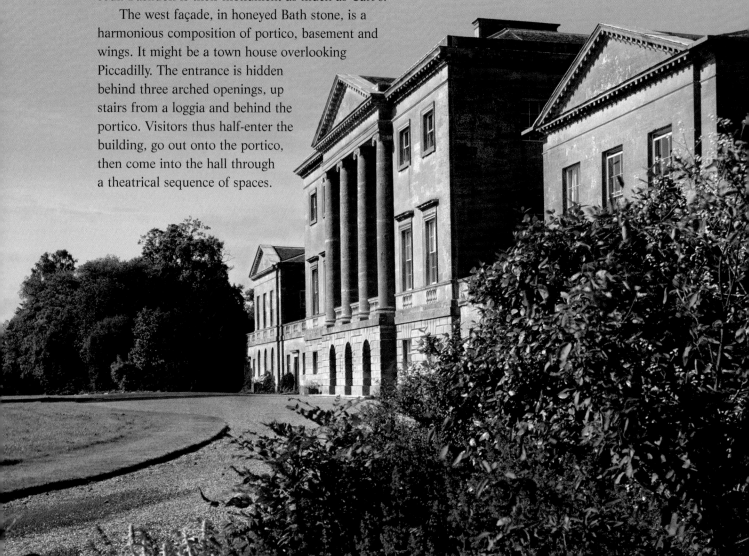

Above To restore the Dining Room at Basildon Park to its 18th-century appearance, the chimneypiece and doorcases were taken from a contemporary Carr house – Panton Hall in Lincolnshire – that had fallen derelict. **Below** The Crimson Bedroom is furnished with a magnificent canopied four-poster bed and matching curtains, dated to c1829, that were originally in Ashburnham Place, Sussex.

Carr's interiors are more refined than, for instance, in his flamboyant Fairfax House in York. They closely reflect the style of Robert Adam, with whom Carr had worked at Harewood House, West Yorkshire. This can immediately be seen in the Etruscan ceiling panels and wall medallions of the hall. The room is as Carr left it, including the superbly crafted doors. The plasterwork is picked out in soft pastel shades of lilac, pale ochre, pink and green.

Carr's plan is based on the dramatic sequence of entrance hall leading direct into the staircase hall and then to the Octagon Saloon and its vista over the park beyond. The stair is light, cantilevered from the wall with delicate treads and iron balusters, a stair up which to glide rather than climb. The Octagon Saloon has a large Venetian window forming a proscenium to the view, hung with drapes like stage curtains. The paintings from the Iliffe collection are mostly works by Batoni, in unusual devotional vein.

The dining room is a perfect example of Carr's deference to Adam. There is a screen of columns at one end and medallions, fronds and tendrils coating every space. The room is also a triumph of meticulous restoration. In the Green Drawing Room, the ceiling takes the form of a wheel of tendrils flanked by heads of Roman emperors.

Upstairs bedrooms contain four-posters, furniture and pictures collected by Lady Iliffe at country house sales across England. She must have had fun. A side room is devoted to Graham Sutherland's cartoons for his great Coventry Cathedral tapestry.

Bear Wood

 A Victorian pile built in neo-Elizabethan style

Near Winnersh, 3 miles SW of Reading; private house, open by arrangement

The Victorian proprietor of *The Times*, John Walter, was a very rich man. By the time he had finished the monstrously extravagant Bear Wood he was not, and *The Times* had eventually to be sold to Lord Northcliffe. Walter was an assiduous commoner. He avoided the company of aristocrats, was philanthropic, religious and refused all honours. He was also an amateur engineer, obsessed with technology. Bear Wood, begun in 1865, is Elizabethan in style, yet was packed with iron and concrete, central heating and fireproofing. It had running water, its own gasworks and five bathrooms.

The house was supposed to have been designed by William Burn, but when Walter read *The English Gentleman's House* by a self-promoting Scotsman, Robert Kerr, he cancelled Burn's contract and commissioned Kerr instead. It was a bad mistake. The building took the rest of the 1860s to complete and the cost was astronomical, some £120,000, draining the coffers of *The Times* to the fury of the staff. The house later became a Merchant Navy orphanage and is now a school dedicated to naval children. The Walter family still live on the estate, although most of their original 7,000 acres have disappeared into Wokingham suburbia.

The building is approached along a sensational avenue of Wellingtonias, one of the most dramatic I know. Driving down it on a windy day is like running the gauntlet of a regiment in fur coats. Its climax is

'The style is **chaotic,** an architectural **doodle.**'

Kerr's huge staircase tower, bristling with pinnacles. Mark Girouard comments that Bear Wood was Kerr's attempt to make Elizabethan seem as 'muscular' as Tractarian Gothic. The result is 'a sock on the jaw ... as if Highclere had been sent on a weightlifting course'. To Pevsner, 'Bear Wood is indeed nearer to Blenheim than to our poky villas'.

The style is chaotic, an architectural doodle. A giant *porte-cochère* fronts a tower with a Belgian roof. On the right is an Elizabethan wing with large gable and projecting window bay. The answering bay on the left is interrupted by the staircase tower, its façade crammed with stepped windows and crowded pilasters. Beyond is a range culminating in the Kitchen Court, with its own gables and tower. The garden front has had the Continental 17th century thrown at it, with projecting bays, towers and Dutch gables.

The interior was one of the largest of any house of the period. The entrance is into what may be considered a screens passage, with the Great Hall to the left. The screen is neo-

Jacobean and the Great Hall is coated in tooled leather. Giant arches lead to the staircase hall. This is more impressive inside than out; indeed, it ranks as a wonder of mid-Victorian architecture, now restored. The stairs rise through two storeys, the ceiling dark blue with stars and brilliantly lit by the tinted glass of the upper windows. The balusters are of Elizabethan pillars on a scrollwork base. Stained glass fills the windows and busts the window sills.

Behind the Great Hall is a large picture gallery. The original pair of drawing rooms run the full depth of the house, divided by sliding doors. These doors are decorated with exquisite marquetry, apparently done on the estate. The panels depict musical instruments surrounded by arabesques. The Renaissance fireplaces have collage overmantels. Upstairs the Bachelors' Rooms and the Young Ladies' Rooms were separate, reached by individual staircases. So too were the Strangers' Menservants' rooms. This fastidious arrangement is also found in Victorian Lanhydrock, in Cornwall.

Englefield house

 Victorianized Elizabethan house with Georgian interiors

At Englefield, 5 miles W of Reading; private house, open by arrangement, gardens open part year

Englefield was owned by Elizabeth I's spy and trusty courtier, Sir Francis Walsingham, whose daughter married the doomed Earl of Essex. It passed through the Paulet family to the present owners, the Benyons. Above the front door are the armorial bearings of a young Paulet who fell in love with and married a servant girl on the estate. Since she had no heraldry of her own, he represented her on his shield in the most romantic fashion, as a simple field of pure gold. She remains thus commemorated to this day.

The house is Walsingham's Elizabethan mansion much rebuilt and reinterpreted by the Georgians, Victorians and the present day. The principal remodelling in the mid-19th century yielded the present romantic outline, a forest of turrets, spikes, cupolas and balustrades, almost a miniature of neighbouring Highclere Castle, in Hampshire. Yet the house is still in form the same house as appears in the background of Nathaniel Dance's portrait of Paulet Wrighte in 1775, which hangs in the house, a classic depiction of an English gentleman and his seat.

The estate is now sandwiched between the A4 and the M4, protected by a park dotted with Victorian estate buildings. The interior is full of Victorian self-confidence. The entrance

hall is of two storeys, with a balcony looking down from the bedroom passage above.

A long corridor links the four main reception rooms to the spacious staircase. Each is stylistically different. The 1770s dining room is brilliant in Corinthian white on plum-coloured walls. Brackets carry the Benyon collection of porcelain beneath a ceiling of Georgian Rococo. The library is heavier, of the 1860s, with bird medallions incorporated into its ceiling. Over the fireplace is a Constable of the house, originally painted with cattle in the foreground but later overpainted with stags to give a more noble setting.

The Victorian drawing room was quietly refreshed by David Mlinaric in the 1980s. Upstairs is a restored Long Gallery, dating from the original Elizabethan house and hung with Restoration portraits. Englefield is an ingenious place, showing every age of English architecture living at ease with the 21st century.

Above The dining room was part of Paulet Wrighte's remodelling of Englefield House in the 1770s. The original plasterwork decoration of the room is now complemented by a set of recently commissioned wall brackets that display the porcelain collection.

Eton college

★★ Famous public school founded in the middle ages

Near Windsor, 2 miles SW of Slough; private house, open part year

Eton may be world famous but at its core is still a simple medieval property of gatehouse, chapel, hall and two courtyards. The old school was founded by Henry VI in 1440, to give seventy scholars a free education and display holy relics, including pieces of the True Cross and the Crown of Thorns. It was thus to be a centre of pilgrimage, with a large pilgrimage church and community of secular priests as well as an almshouse. The original college took some eighty years to complete, by when the appeal of relics was giving way to the forces of Reformation. The scholastic role went from strength to strength.

The outer courtyard, School Yard, contains the original scholars' buildings and the chapel, the only one of the original buildings to be of stone. The yard forms an intimate campus, still with a medieval atmosphere. The range to the street was rebuilt in the 17th century because it was falling down. On the upper floor is Upper School, a Restoration classroom, its panelling covered with boys' names carved into the wood. To the left of School Yard is Lower School, reputedly the oldest schoolroom in the world, in continuous use since 1443. Its heavy beams and pillars give it the appearance of a ship below decks. Again the carving of initials is much in evidence.

Above For 200 years, the Lower School was Eton's only classroom. According to accounts of 16th-century life at Eton, scholars began lessons here at 6.00am.

Right A second classroom, the Upper School, was built in the 17th century when a western range was added to School Yard by Provost Allestree. The first structure, constructed in 1665, proved to be unsafe and had to be rebuilt in 1689.

At the far side of School Yard is Lupton's Tower, leading to the cloisters, College Hall and Provost's Lodge. These are also shown to the public. The Hall has scissorbeams above a Victorian screen coated in Etonian heraldry. The library and the adjacent museum of Eton life are minor gems. The library was constructed when the cloisters were raised a floor in 1729, in an early Georgian style with a gallery. It comprises three interconnecting rooms beneath a rich classical ceiling. Among its treasures is a Gutenberg Bible.

Welford park

★ 17th-century mansion, much altered in the 19th century

At Welford, 6 miles NW of Newbury; private house, open part year

'... the setting **appears** to date
from the house's **monastic origins.**'

The house is close to its village in the French style. Outbuildings are contiguous with cottages and the church, while the entrance faces outwards towards the fields. This setting appears to date from the house's monastic origins.

Welford Park was owned by the Archer family and the building dates from the mid-17th century. The current owners, the Puxleys, are tortuously descended from the Archers and also from the Newtons of Lincolnshire. Isaac Newton, of humble origins, was keen to declare his kinship with them. Later, when he was famous, they were keen to claim kinship with him. The Newton male line died out, however, when a baby son and heir was carelessly thrown out of a window by the family monkey. All this is recorded in a fine collection of family portraits hanging in the house.

The house was designed by John Jackson of Oxford. There is much English bond brickwork on the side elevations. The history of the main elevation is vexed and has been attributed to the architect Thomas Archer, briefly married into the family, but the way the pilasters meet the corners is botched and the pediment seems unrelated. It is barely conceivable a proper architect can have been involved – or at least there must have been a fearful row.

The interior of Welford was much altered in the 1830s and remains in family use. Apart from some curious Rococo pelmets, the chief interest is a magnificent John Wootton painting of a hunting scene which dominates the stairwell.

Right In the 1830s, the interiors at Welford were remodelled around a stairwell rising the full height of the house. The staircase itself dates from a much earlier programme of building, c1695, when the house was much improved and the staircase sited in what is now the north wing. It was moved to its new position in the 19th-century development, one of the few important late 17th-century features to have survived.

Windsor castle

★ ★ ★ ★ ☆ Archetypal royal castle, home of English monarchs since William the Conqueror

At Windsor, 3 miles SW of Slough; museum, open all year

Overlooking the Thames at Windsor is one of the finest palaces in the world. Few English people visit Windsor Castle because they think of it as the private residence of the Queen. That indeed applies to over a third of the floor area. But this place is gigantic. Nowhere in England is as regal as Windsor, not even Hampton Court. It is the supreme expression of monarchy in architecture and art.

The castle is clearly visible from the M4 where it sits directly under the Heathrow flightpath. The castle was founded by William the Conqueror, who built the present Round Tower on the mound by the Upper Ward. Edward III built a large medieval palace round it, with the knightly precinct of the College of St George in the Lower Ward. Windsor was a Parliamentary stronghold in the Civil War.

Two great periods of expansion followed. First was under the epic builder, Charles II, for whom Hugh May constructed the state apartments in the 1670s. These interiors were decorated by Antonio Verrio and Grinling Gibbons. This range was then vastly extended by George III and George IV. Their architects were James

Wyatt and his nephew, Jeffry Wyatville, designing in the Picturesque style. They gave Windsor a grand suite of neo-Gothic ceremonial and banqueting chambers, as well as semi-state entertaining rooms adjacent to the Royal Family's private quarters. They raised the Round Tower by a storey and added subsidiary towers, gates, terraces and staircases. It is principally to Wyatville that we owe the Castle's present outline.

The guidebook to Windsor is exemplary, including a plan of the furnishing and pictures in each room. The entrance to the state and semi-state rooms is from the North Terrace, leading into Wyatt's Gothic undercroft. This now houses the Dolls' House, and galleries displaying drawings by Leonardo, Michelangelo and others. It also serves as the formal entrance to the Grand Staircase and Grand Vestibule.

The staircase, further altered by Salvin, borders on the kitsch. It presents the English monarch as a figure of Arthurian, if not Wagnerian, romance. Mounted knights in armour flank the ascent. A great Gothic lantern rises overhead. The visitor emerges into a series of vestibules, all wallowing in armour, trophies, swords, guns and shields. In one is the gold tiger's head captured from the throne of the Indian Tippoo Sahib and the lead bullet which killed Nelson. The fan-vaulted Grand Vestibule is a temple to armorial glory.

Beyond is the Waterloo Chamber, intended by George IV to commemorate the final defeat of Napoleon. It is hung with the twenty portraits of allied European leaders involved

'... one of the **finest palaces** in the **world**.'

27

Right The King's Dining Room is part of Charles II's suite of state rooms. It is dominated by a ceiling painting, *The Banquet of the Gods,* by Verrio. Original carvings by Grinling Gibbons and Henry Phillips adorn the walls. **Below** The Waterloo Chamber was constructed in the 1820s specifically to display the Lawrence portraits commissioned by George IV. These depict the statesmen and monarchs involved in Napoleon's defeat and include portraits of Marshal von Blücher, the Duke of Wellington and Pope Pius VII.

in Wellington's last campaign, all by Sir Thomas Lawrence. The roof is said to have been shaped to reflect the timbers of a ship. The panels separating the portraits are salvaged work of Grinling Gibbons. This is a stupendous room.

The visitor now enters Charles II's state rooms. They are arranged as the King's and Queen's rooms, with decoration to match, and contain many of the finest pictures from the Royal Collection. The King's Drawing Room is almost all Rubens. The bed chamber is Canaletto and Gainsborough, with a magnificent French 'polonaise' bed. The dressing room has works by Steen, Rembrandt, Holbein and van Dyck. The closet has William Hogarth's charming *Garrick with his Wife*.

The Queen's Drawing Room and the King's Dining Room contain Holbeins and other royal portraits. The latter carries superb carved panels by Grinling Gibbons, flanking French tapestries and a ceiling by Verrio. The Queen's Ballroom is by Wyatville, with silver furniture and massive canvasses by van Dyck. With the Queen's Audience and Presence Chambers, the visitor returns to the Restoration at its most voluptuous. No inch of wall or ceiling is without

painting or tapestry, including four massive Gobelins and ceilings by Verrio.

At this point, the Queen's Guard Chamber comes as a relief, with its Wyatville Gothic vault and a return to displays of swords and muskets. Here is an exhibition of thrones, including two by Morris and Co. In the centre sits a chair of state of pure ivory; it was presented to Queen Victoria by the Maharajah of Travancore.

The tour now passes into St George's Hall, the site of Edward III's hall for the Garter Knights. The Hall was refashioned by Wyatville in 1829 and radically refashioned after the fire in 1992 which destroyed the hall and adjacent chapel and a number of the state and semi-state rooms beyond. The restoration of the hall was controversial, some critics demanding a modernist interpretation.

The chosen style – not quite a facsimile – might be termed 1990s conservator's Gothic, the latest in a long line of such fantasies at Windsor. It is a place of armoured knights and exotic lighting, with the King's Champion on a horse riding into

Above On 20 November 1992, a fire broke out in the Private Chapel at Windsor, started by a lamp left too close to a curtain. The Grand Reception Room was one of the most badly damaged rooms. Now restored to its former gilded splendour, the chamber is home to a series of large Gobelins tapestries, gifts from Charles X of France to William IV, that fortunately survived the conflagration.

space from the minstrel's gallery like a character from *The Lord of the Rings*. The ceiling panels are the arms of the Garter Knights, blank ones representing those who 'fell from grace'.

Beyond the hall, state rooms become semi-state ones, comprehensively and lavishly restored after the fire. The turn takes place in the Lantern Lobby, on the site of the destroyed chapel. Its ecclesiastical form was based by the architects, Sidell Gibson, on the crossing of Ely Cathedral and, so I am told, the Abbey of Batalha outside Lisbon. The semi-state rooms are open only in winter. They were designed by Wyatville for George IV and include the Green Drawing Room and sumptuous Crimson Drawing Room. In sequence beyond is the State Dining Room, still in use, and the smaller Gothic Octagon Dining Room. The windows from here give onto the private gardens. At this point, Windsor is almost intimate.

Yet it saves its final flourish to last, the Grand Reception Room. Here the taste is French Empire for George IV. Wyatville protested at the rejection of his preferred Gothic but was overruled by the King. The panelling was brought from Paris as a backdrop to massive Gobelins tapestries. The ceiling is a post-fire reproduction. Beyond is the Garter Throne Room, where investitures take place. The exit is past the Waterloo Chamber and out into the Upper Ward quadrangle. It is a breathtaking and exhausting promenade. And this is a small part of the castle. The east and south ranges are private to the Royal Family.

Queen Mary's Dolls' house

★ Meticulous re-creation in miniature of a royal residence, on show at Windsor Castle

The house was planned in 1921 as a gift to Queen Mary, to designs by Sir Edwin Lutyens. It stands (8½ft wide and 5ft tall) and is displayed in a darkened chamber, the exterior walls of the house lifted up to reveal its interior. So perfect is the miniaturization that within minutes we seem to be in a 'real' house, on a scale of 1 to 12. The eye perambulates. It wanders through halls, bedrooms, kitchens and garages alive with a 'pretend' royal family at work and play. The intention was 'to show future generations how a king and queen of England lived in the 20th century'.

The Dolls' House project involved the skills of 1,500 people. Everything works. We are told that the gramophone plays, the wine in the bottles is vintage, the lifts go up and down, the water runs, the bed linen is of the best and every light is wired with electricity. Kipling, Hardy, Graves, Belloc, Chesterton and others wrote the tiny volumes in the library. Orpen, Flint, Nicholson and Gertler contributed pictures. In the presses are 700 original drawings. It must be the world's most exquisite toy, using microscopic crafts-manship where a Russian Tsar would have lavished jewels.

The exterior is in what Lutyens called his 'Wrenaissance' style. The window sashes operate smoothly. The garden was designed by Gertrude Jekyll although the flowers are not real, a lapse. There is even a ring of toadstools, hiding a snail and butterflies. In the basement garage are

Above The Dolls' House was kept in Lutyens' own home until 1924, when it was packed up and sent to the British Empire Exhibition, and then to its present home at Windsor Castle.

models of the most luxurious cars of the day, including a Rolls-Royce, Daimler, Lanchester and a Rudge motor cycle.

The interior is not of a palace but rather of a luxurious country house. There is no suite of state rooms or royal receiving rooms, merely a saloon, library and dining room. The Lutyens' touch is the marble front hall (with precisely crafted men in armour) and sweeping staircase. The triumph of the ground floor is the library, with books, pictures, prints, globes and even a pair of Purdey shotguns. In the dining room the ceiling pattern is repeated in the carpet. There is a real Munnings over the mantelpiece. The butler's pantry next door contains Crown Jewels in the strong-room. The saloon piano is by Broadwood and plays.

The bathrooms are astonishing: the king's bathroom is of green marble, the queen's of alabaster with silver taps. The maids' rooms are no less carefully depicted, as are the kitchen and other offices in the basement. Nothing seems to have been omitted, not even the corks in the bottles, the tiny dolls in the day nursery, the golf clubs in the bag.

To what purpose is this absurd detail, assembled at vast expense and most of it invisible to the naked eye? The answer is to excite wonder, which it does. We leave the house past a gallery of 'real' dolls with their trousseaux, given by the French government in 1938 to Queen Mary's granddaughters, the princesses Elizabeth and Margaret. These dolls look like giants.

London

London Central

Apsley house

✦✦ The Duke of Wellington's London home, museum of Napoleonic trophies and treasures

Hyde Park Corner, London W1; English Heritage, open all year

Each year after the anniversary of the Battle of Waterloo, Wellington would hold a banquet in his London house for his surviving officers. On the walls hung masterpieces which the French had looted from Madrid and which Wellington had recaptured and been given in thanks by the King of Spain. Down the centre of the dining table ran the stupendous silver service of 1,000 pieces which Wellington had also been given as a thank-you by the Portuguese. Its centrepiece shows four continents dancing in joy round fasces representing the allies. This annual reminder of England's past glory drew huge crowds to Hyde Park Corner to witness the heroes arriving in their carriages.

'The house was known (and still is to taxi drivers) as Number One, London.'

The house was known (and still is to taxi drivers) as Number One, London. It had been built in 1771 by Robert Adam for Baron Apsley, Lord Chancellor and later 2nd Earl Bathurst. In 1807, the 3rd Earl sold the house to the Marquess Wellesley, who in 1817 sold it to his brother, Wellington. At that time, Wellington was launching himself on a political career. He had Benjamin Dean Wyatt turn the Adam town house into a Regency palace. Grandeur took the place of domesticity, neo-classical coldness for Adam warmth. Wyatt added gates, a portico and galleries. The impact of this work was ruined in the 1960s, with the demolition of houses to the east and the building of a dual carriageway and modern hotel in their place. The building now stands isolated, classical and rather sombre.

Apsley House was given to the nation in 1947. While the family retained the upper floor, the *piano nobile* has become little more than an art gallery. Moves are afoot to give the main rooms more the feel of a house, although Apsley House was always essentially for show. The Wellington memorabilia complements the collections at Stratfield Saye, Hampshire, and Walmer Castle, Kent, where the Duke died.

The downstairs rooms are crammed with statues, busts, plate and porcelain, including the great Wellington Shield. A pictorial reconstruction of Waterloo by Felix Philipotteaux well illustrates 'the fog of battle'. In the stairwell stands a bizarre statue of Napoleon as a Greek athlete, naked but for a figleaf. Although by Canova, Napoleon disliked it for lacking his 'calm dignity'. It was bought by the British government and presented to the Duke.

The upstairs rooms form a grand circuit. The Piccadilly Drawing Room survives from the Adam house, with an apse at one end and Adam's ceiling decoration in white and gold. The paintings are mostly Dutch genre, including a de Hooch and works by Teniers. Also by Adam is the Portico Drawing Room, once completing the west side of the house.

Apsley House now changes from West End town house to latter day Blenheim. The Waterloo Gallery was added by Wyatt in triumphal style. Windows, cornices and ceiling panels are heavy and ornate, coated in gold leaf and with rich red hangings. The pictures, from the Spanish prize, include Velasquez's *Waterseller* and works by van Dyck and Rubens.

The remainder of the Adam rooms were altered beyond recognition by Wyatt. The Yellow and Striped Drawing Rooms were converted from Adam's Etruscan Room and state bedroom, a sad loss. The latter contains a flourish of military portraits and landscapes. The final room is the dining room, the setting for the Waterloo Banquets. It is eerily empty without its heroes.

Duke of Wellington
1769–1852

Arthur Wellesley was born in Dublin into an aristocratic Irish family. He made his career in the army and was awarded the title Duke of Wellington after his victories in the Peninsular War, which drove the French forces from Spain and contributed to the initial defeat of Napoleon in 1814. When Napoleon escaped from Elba and returned to France in 1815, Wellington took command of the Anglo-Allied forces in the final battle to defeat him. Victory at Waterloo made Wellington a hero and he returned to Britain and a career in politics; he became Prime Minister in 1828. On his death, he was honoured with a state funeral and interred in St Paul's Cathedral.

Banqueting house

The Banqueting House was the London stage on which the Stuart dynasty acted out the 17th century. Created by James I, it witnessed the death of his son, the Restoration of one grandson, the usurpation of another, James II, and the formal offer of the Crown by Parliament to his granddaughter, Mary. Today, it is the only complete fragment of what was once the grandest and most important of London's royal palaces. The former York Place was the home of Cardinal Wolsey, from whom it was seized along with Hampton Court by Henry VIII. It succeeded the old Palace of Westminster as chief residence of the Tudor and Stuart monarchs and was, to Macaulay, 'the most celebrated palace in which the sovereigns of England have ever dwelt'.

In reality, Whitehall was a jumble of buildings erected as and when money was available. The mostly Tudor reception rooms could not handle large occasions, which therefore called for separate premises. Elizabeth erected temporary pavilions for entertainment and it was one of these that James I rebuilt to a new 'Italian' design by Inigo Jones in 1619. The building was studiously Palladian, a double cube with a ceiling painted by Rubens, and was Jones's second work in this style after the Queen's House in Greenwich (see page 96).

The splendour of the Banqueting House stimulated Charles I to plan a new riverside palace to rival the Louvre, a fantasy that was to consume the ambition of his son. Plans were prepared by Jones and his pupil, John Webb, but curtailed by the Civil War. In 1649, the Banqueting House saw its most celebrated moment in the trial of Charles himself and his execution outside. Under the Commonwealth, Whitehall Palace fell into decay and its treasures were dispersed. The Banqueting House narrowly escaped destruction.

The palace plan was revived by Charles II and put in hand by Sir Christopher Wren. But the King was building palaces across England and this work was not commenced. Two fires, in 1691 and 1698, consumed most of the old buildings and the Court moved to St James's Palace, never to return. The Banqueting House survived and was left alone, towering over Whitehall in paintings of the period like a magnificent ship beached on the banks of the river. It became a Chapel Royal and then a military museum.

The Banqueting House is now overshadowed by the 20th-century Ministry of Defence while the radicalism of Jones's design is diluted by the monumental buildings of Whitehall. Its Italian Palladianism is no longer an exception in overwhelmingly classical Westminster.

The façade to Whitehall is of seven bays, the centre three divided by attached columns, the outer ones by pilasters. Two equal storeys of windows light what is just one chamber inside. The entablatures, enriched with swags, are complex and Baroque. It is all a beautifully controlled composition, having what Pevsner called 'sobriety, gravity and learning'. But so subsequently has most of Whitehall.

Above Rubens visited the Banqueting House in around 1630 when Charles I commissioned him to paint the ceiling. The panels were painted in Antwerp, then shipped to London at the end of 1635. Rubens never saw the work *in situ*.

The Main Hall inside is reached up a new staircase added to the north end by James Wyatt in 1809. It is a vast, empty chamber, the two storeys of windows divided by a sumptuous balcony running round the room. There would have been no furniture, the room being filled with people, but the walls were once adorned with the Royal collection of tapestries. Today, all eyes turn to Rubens' ceiling installed in 1636, on the theme of the Apotheosis of James I. It promotes the divinity of kings and depicts the monarch commanding, variously, Justice, Zeal, Religion, Honour, Peace, Plenty, Rebellion, Greed and Lust. There is no Jonesian sobriety or gravity here, only Baroque exuberance and boasting.

Buckingham palace

★★★ Regency palatial splendour in the heart of the capital

The Mall, London SW1; private house, open part year

The fire that broke out in Windsor Castle in November 1992 had a silver lining. For decades, Buckingham Palace had resisted requests to admit the public. Now, to help pay for repairs to Windsor, doors were thrown open. Tours were allowed of the Regency state rooms and England's most famous house was accessible at last.

The palace has never enjoyed public affection, regularly appearing in 'least-loved building' league tables. The early 20th-century façade is dull, while the Palladian front to the garden is hidden by walls festooned with security devices. Yet 'The Palace' symbolizes the British monarchy, as 'Downing Street' symbolizes government. The approach down The Mall to the Victoria Memorial is London's one flourish of imperial grandeur. The celebrated railings and the Changing of the Guard are steeped in British history.

While the palace does not equal Windsor or Hampton Court in grandeur, its interiors designed by John Nash for George IV are the most opulent in London. They also contain some of the monarch's most spectacular paintings, rotated with those displayed in the new Queen's Gallery off Buckingham Palace Road. No private apartments are seen. A visit is like a peep into a museum of royalty. We see a throne but no bed.

The former house on the site was built by, and named after, the Dukes of Buckingham in the early 18th century. It was bought in 1760 by George III as a semi-rural retreat from the court ceremonial of adjacent St James's Palace, to which foreign ambassadors are still accredited. George IV commissioned Nash to rebuild Buckingham House, intending to move the entire court from St James's, but he never lived to occupy it.

Nash had a terrible time with Buckingham Palace. There was never enough money and Parliament baulked at the expense of what the King was demanding. Nash decided to keep the old house as a core and attached new reception rooms when money allowed. He added flanking wings for private apartments and enclosed the courtyard with Marble Arch. This was moved to the north-east corner of Hyde Park by the Victorians, who replaced it with an extra range of guestrooms, regrettably enclosing the entrance courtyard. This Victorian wing, by Edward Blore, was given a Portland stone façade by Sir Aston Webb in 1913, completed while George V was away on holiday. It complemented Webb's Admiralty Arch at the other end of The Mall.

Above The rear façade of Buckingham Palace looks out over lawns, snow-covered here but in summer the scene of the Queen's famous garden parties. **Below** The Grand Staircase was one of the most extravagant of George IV's additions to the palace. The balusters were commissioned from the craftsman Samuel Parker; made in 1828–30 in cast and gilded bronze, they cost £3,900.

Nash's palace behind is in warm Bath stone, entered under a *porte-cochère* into the 'rustic' floor of the former house. Nash capitalized brilliantly on this modesty by making the staircase rise to his *piano nobile*, as if from the underworld up to Heaven. This staircase is the best thing in the Palace. It forms a Baroque curve with gilded bronze balusters sweeping upwards beneath portraits by Lawrence, Beechey and Wilkie. From here sheer opulence takes over. Only state rooms are on show, their style reflecting George's love of 'French Empire'. Occasionally, frigid classicism is warmed by an abundance of regal red. Everything is lavishly decorated, sometimes indigestibly so.

Thus the ceiling of the Green Drawing Room is a swirl of circles above coving that drips with gilt. The Throne Room has a proscenium backed by red silk walls and a canopy over the state chairs, a scene more appropriate for an oriental potentate. Down the spine of the building is the Picture Gallery (described in the palace guide as being like an ocean liner). Here the stars

ceilings. The Blue Drawing Room is filled with scagliola columns rising to giant brackets, while the ceiling rains gilt on guests below. High up are plaster reliefs of Shakespeare, Milton and Spenser. In the middle of the enfilade is the bow-windowed Music Room. It is a charming pavilion, with domed ceiling and lapis lazuli scagliola columns. This is where royal babies are traditionally baptized. The White Drawing Room beyond is more feminine. White walls rise through giant pilasters to a gilded tent-like ceiling. A superb Riesener roll-top desk sits quietly in a corner.

Visitors are ushered out down the Ministers' Staircase and into the garden through the Oval Room, conduit for guests heading for Palace garden parties. Here are two charming portraits of the young Victoria and Albert by Winterhalter. From the garden, the view of Buckingham Palace is almost a shock, so unlike the stately Mall façade. It is that of a comfortable, rather unpretentious, country home, which is what that decent man, George III, had intended before his son began spending so much money.

are the pictures, works by van Dyck, Rembrandt, Rubens, Guercino, Poussin, Canaletto and the Queen's lovely Vermeer of *The Music Lesson*. There is something calming in Vermeer's domestic allegory amid all this ceremony of state.

The sequence of reception rooms loses a sense of crescendo because visitors cannot view them as intended, leading to the (inaccessible) Great Ballroom. Each is best regarded as an individual explosion of Nash extravagance. The state dining room is a voluptuous display of red and gilt with Nash's ceiling imitating the Brighton Pavilion. Three grand reception rooms overlook the garden, all with astonishing

Cabinet war rooms

⭐ Churchill's wartime bunker

Clive Steps, King Charles Street, London SW1;
museum, open all year

Above The sand-bagged entrance to the Cabinet War Rooms is at one side of Clive Steps in Whitehall. **Left** At the heart of a labyrinth of underground offices and corridors lies Churchill's operational command centre, the Map Room.

'This is the room from which I will direct the war,' said Churchill in 1940 as he inspected the basement under the New Public Offices in Whitehall. The rooms had been shielded from bomb attack by a thick membrane of concrete, still visible in the wall facing St James's Park. When the war was over, someone turned off the lights and the entire area was left undisturbed, as if awaiting another war. Only in 1981 did Margaret Thatcher decree that it be opened as a museum. It is now run by the Imperial War Museum, with an attached Churchill Museum.

The warren of rooms on display are linked by submarine-like corridors. Everything is strictly functional, with pipes and wires exposed and frequent bossy notices. The sounds of ringing phones and footsteps can be heard, a voice barks an order to 'Stop that whistling'. A distant siren wails, a reminder of the wartime world that would have been above. An effigy of Churchill sits in the Transatlantic Telephone Room, actually a converted broom cupboard. The phone line connected to the US via the 'Sigsaly' message scrambler hidden deep beneath Selfridges in Oxford Street.

The rooms were completely self-contained and in use round the clock. A sign tells the staff whether it is sun or rain outside. This is mostly a habitation of secretaries and clerks, their camp beds and typewriters still in place. One wrote that 'even in this revolting place called "the dock", one could get a good night's sleep because you didn't hear the bombs raining down'.

At the heart of operations lies the Map Room, with a connecting door to Churchill's bedroom. (He preferred to risk Downing Street to sleep, but by 1941 had been persuaded to stay underground during air raids.) The desk dominates the room, covered in phones of many colours. Today, they are manned by wax effigies, one from each branch of the armed services. Microphones were linked to the BBC and maps still paper the walls. Never was the maxim more evident, that 'war is primarily about maps'.

Carlyle's house

★★ Chelsea home of Victorian sage and writer

24 Cheyne Row, London SW3; National Trust, open part year

Why Carlyle's Chelsea home should have been so venerated is something of a mystery. He was chiefly known for two biographies of then unfashionable figures, Cromwell and Frederick the Great, and for his publicly unsociable marriage, revealed in his wife, Jane's, correspondence. Yet as the guidebook says, 'Soon after his arrival in London he became and remained an object of social curiosity. His venerable appearance, his utter independence, his doom-laden view of the folly and triviality of the world, his powerful and idiosyncratic command of language and his renowned ability to speak for hours at a time were all manifestations of genius to which the Victorian imagination readily responded.' Perhaps his unhappy marriage added an element of spice. It was exacerbated, according to a contemporary, 'by the exceptional intellect and character of the persons involved'.

The house had been built in 1708 on land running south from the banks of the Thames. The Carlyles arrived from Scotland in 1834. Chelsea was not then a smart suburb and the house was by Victorian standards modest. Jane Carlyle was intelligent, sociable and a most talented correspondent. The couple lived here for thirty-two years. A painting in the house, *A Chelsea Interior* by Robert Tait, shows the couple at home in an attitude of frozen domestic hostility.

Jane died in 1866 and Thomas in 1881. A public subscription was at once launched to purchase the house as a museum, now run by the National Trust. Since London is short of terrace houses open to the public this is a blessing. The exterior is that of a typical Queen Anne terraced house, of three main floors plus attic and basement, with cheery white woodwork. The interior is said to be as

Above left Large folding doors link the front parlour to the back dining room where the Carlyles took their breakfast. This in turn opens onto the china closet, a room that Carlyle described as 'fit to hold crockery for the whole street'. **Bottom left** A carbon photograph of Thomas Carlyle (1795–1881), taken in 1865. **Left** Jane Carlyle's dressing room is furnished with a marble-topped washstand which she bought with £5 that Thomas gave her for Christmas in 1850. The towel rail and hip-bath were originally in her husband's dressing room.
Above Seeking silence in which to work, in 1853 Carlyle commissioned a sound-proof attic study. A new staircase was built to provide access, with a narrow closet at either end, and an air-chamber was constructed in the roof for light. Unfortunately for Carlyle, these features served to amplify noises from the river.

the couple left it, overwhelmingly brown and rather lugubrious, perhaps reflecting Carlyle's view of the world.

The ground floor parlour was often used by Carlyle as a study. Its redecoration caused the last of his 'domestic earthquakes' with Jane shortly before her death. Downstairs is the kitchen, with the maid's cot by the stove. Upstairs is the library, with Carlyle's chair and bookcase and Morris willow-pattern wallpaper. To the rear is Jane's bedroom, a poignant chamber with a small dressing room beyond. Here we read of her suffering 'more sorrows

than are common' and of a marriage afflicted by 'irritation, frustration, resentment and jealousy'.

The attic was Carlyle's study until he was too distracted by noise from the river. It is now a museum of memorabilia, every wall covered in pictures, prints and austere photographs of the pair. The house is still blessed with its garden. This overlooked meadows when the Carlyles arrived, with the Tudor wall of old Shrewsbury House as the boundary. Here Carlyle wrote that he could 'wander about in dressing-gown and straw hat, as of old, and take my pipe in peace in it'. He could do so today.

Dartmouth house

⭐ Aristocratic Mayfair house built in the French style

37 Charles Street, London W1; private house,
open by arrangement

Below The exterior ironwork is echoed on the staircase
leading to the reception rooms on the first floor. Overlooking
Charles Street is the Small Drawing Room, which features an
Italian *pietra-dura*-style fireplace.

Squeezed behind two Georgian façades is a house rebuilt in 1890 for the banker Edward Baring, 1st Lord Revelstoke. It is a *fin de siècle* West End house in the French manner, designed to seem grander than its proportions suggest. Subsequently acquired by the 6th Earl of Dartmouth, it is now the English Speaking Union club, viewable on polite application.

The architect was W. Allwright, who gave the exterior a Baroque overlay of wayward pediments and florid ironwork. The interiors were primarily designed to show off Baring's French furniture. The entrance and main reception room are in Louis XIV style, with a Wedgwood Room to the right. This is blue and white with highly decorated panels and cherubic overmantels after designs by François Boucher.

The staircase might be that of an *hôtel* on a Paris *grand boulevard*. Marble treads rise between voluptuous iron and bronze balusters past a large Venetian window. The walls are decorated with Baroque plasterwork and the ceiling is what Pevsner called 'chocolate-box Tiepolo'. The walnut-lined ballroom upstairs is particularly extrovert, its panelling a 1740s import from elsewhere. The fireplace came from Robert Adam's Derby House in Grosvenor Square.

Dennis Severs house

★★★★ Fantasy re-creation of an 18th-century silk weaver's family home

18 Folgate Street, London E1; private house, open part year

I approach this house with trepidation. It stands in a surreal, 18th-century enclave under the looming cliffs of Bishopsgate, and might be the back lot of a film studio. No.18 Folgate Street is a simple three-bay town house of *c*1724, built of stock bricks with brightly painted ground-floor shutters. It was acquired by an American collector, Dennis Severs, in 1979. He lived in it and filled it with mostly contemporary fittings and antiques, showing them to the public in a strictly controlled fashion. On his death in 1999 he left the house and collection to a local trust.

Severs was more than an eccentric. He presented the house as, variously, an Old Master painting, a still-life drama, an experience, an opera and a peep show. It was not for children, tourists, 'bored wives of company directors', or those who needed guiding or wanted to talk. Visits were and are conducted in silence. The house is also said to be 'post-materialist', Another Time, a spell and a soul.

Strip away the mumbo-jumbo and what do we have? The answer is what almost every house-museum in England is trying to be, while often pretending not to be. Folgate Street seeks to embalm the atmosphere as well as the physical presence of a historic building. Since all such exercises are ersatz, Severs argued, at least do them well. Everything apart from the walls and roof has been imported as appropriate for an early-Georgian residence, including furniture, fittings, doors, even plasterwork. For authenticity, Severs stripped out a bathroom and an upstairs kitchen and ripped away all wiring. Light and heat come from candles and fireplaces. He

Below left A visitor to Dennis Severs House becomes something of a time traveller and the journey begins on the ground floor in the early 18th century. In the candlelit dining room the decor is Georgian and the walls are hung with suitable paintings and artefacts. On the table lies the remains of a meal, with half-empty wine glasses and unsmoked clay pipes.

then invented a silk-weaving couple, the Jervises, with their lodgers and servant, and equipped the house on the basis of his research into how they would have lived.

As well as a house and its people, Severs then created a moment in time, with the visitor as silent spy. The Jervises have just stepped out of the front door, leaving their wine unfinished, their tea cups a mess, cigar smoke in the air and chamber pots unemptied. Rubbish is dumped, as would have been the case, in fireplaces. Candles gutter in the draught. Wigs lie awry. The kitchen is filthy. In Severs' day, a scruffy lodger in 18th-century dress might at any moment clatter downstairs and go out of the door.

The rest is all impressions. On the ground floor, a canary cheeps in the dining room. The walls are hung with clay pipes, shell sconces and (real) game. Memos in the form of scraps of paper are everywhere. The upstairs smoking room is arranged in imitation of the picture over the fireplace. The well-appointed drawing room in front, with pilasters and panelled ceiling, has walnut shells for garlands and silhouettes against the window screens. The second floor has a boudoir, perfumed and with napkins left littering the chairs. In the bedroom, porcelain crowds the walls. The unmade bed still has the indentation of two heads on the pillows, lovingly close. The chamber pot stinks.

The masterpiece is the top floor. The family, clearly on hard times, has taken in two lodgers. The resulting garret is the best evocation of London poverty I know. Grey washing is draped from ropes over the stairs. Walls are peeling, the ceilings falling. Everything is covered in dust, top hats, clothes, books, chairs. Cobwebs decorate corners and windows. The curtains and bed-hangings are so ragged they are falling to the floor. In a corner are the desk and quills of an impecunious clerk.

These rooms smell of damp and desolation. There are gentle sound effects, as of a bird outside or the bells of Spitalfields church. Some visitors leave the room, I am told, in tears. Since the Spitalfields Historic Buildings Trust insists the house be lived in still, 'to provide noises on the stairs', an occupant sleeps in one of the pauper's beds in the rear room, in conditions of candlelit squalor. Where he bathes is a mystery.

The only lapse is back downstairs where Severs created a crowded Victorian parlour, an uncomfortable anachronism apparently because he had also acquired Victoriana in his travels. But Folgate Street is mostly of a piece. Its truth to life defies the scrubbed artificiality of National Trust and English Heritage 'time warps'. It may not be for copying, but there is not a house custodian in England who would not benefit from a visit.

Dickens' house

When the young Charles Dickens moved his family to Doughty Street in 1837 he was elated by the success of the first parts of *Pickwick Papers*. Doughty Street was respectability at last, with gates and liveried gate-keepers to keep out undesirables. The terrace house of the standard London three storeys, with attic and basement, was built in 1807–9. The ground floor windows have shutters, the front door a fanlight. It was a big step up from the cramped quarters off Fleet Street where he had lived as a journalist. He moved in with his wife, Catherine, his son Charley, his brother Fred and Catherine's younger sister, Mary.

For Dickens, Doughty Street was a period of intense, if brief, marital happiness. He stayed here just two years until the growing family forced a move to Regent's Park (the vanished Devonshire Terrace). The house saw the completion of *Pickwick* and the writing of *Oliver Twist* and *Nicholas Nickleby*. Soon after his arrival, Dickens witnessed the sudden death of his adored sister-in-law, Mary, at the age of seventeen. The experience shattered him. Mary's poignant death was to recur in many of his novels, notably that of Little Nell in *The Old Curiosity Shop* also written around this time.

The house was threatened with demolition in 1923 but saved by the Dickens Fellowship and reopened as a museum. Hagiography hangs heavy on the interior. No attempt is made to evoke the hyperactive Dickens, rushing from pillar to post, entertaining his publisher, Bentley, with singing and dramatic imitations. The one half-restored room, the drawing room on the first floor, is protected by an ugly glass screen. The place is a mass of memorabilia, mostly of Dickens' novels and the characters in them.

Upstairs can be seen Dickens' study desk and a copy of *The Empty Chair*, the original painting being at Gad's Hill in Kent. The top rooms are used for exhibitions of Dickensiana. Mary Hogarth lived her brief life in the room at the back. The basement kitchen has become a library and meeting room for the Dickens Fellowship, a suitably Pickwickian use.

This is not so much Dickens' House as a house out of Dickens, a musty shrine where the visitor is asked to wander amid the shades of the departed master and touch the odd stick, hat and newspaper clipping. It badly needs the man himself to burst in and roar the place to life.

Handel house museum

⭐ Composer's Georgian town house

25 Brook Street, London W1; museum, open all year

George Frederic Handel lived in Brook Street for thirty-six of his fifty years in London and died here in 1759. In this simple Georgian terrace town house he composed *The Messiah*, rehearsed, entertained, sold music and concert tickets and led a gregarious, chaotic bachelor existence. He ate gargantuan meals and was the rumbustious life and soul of musical London.

For years the house was occupied by a variety of tenants. Then, rescued in the 1990s, it was opened as a museum in 2001. The custodians ask us to see it as 'not glamorous but a good, honest middle-class home'. Large sums have been spent on research, documentation, lifts, disabled access, metal back stairs, audio-visual aids, video rooms, fancy lighting and everything that health-and-safety regulations could do to eliminate the atmosphere of an old building. I am afraid that Handel's 'home' this is not.

Since the trust was outrageously denied occupation of the ground floor, Handel's 'shop', visitors must go upstairs and start their tour at the top, through an audio-visual display room. This leads into a gallery devoted to Handel's contemporaries and then to his bedroom, stark with a reproduction canopied bed and copy of Hudson's portrait of the composer. Downstairs is the rehearsal room, where students still play Handel on a harpsichord.

The museum is clearly struggling to do well by the great man and is seeking more furniture. But if it could defer to the gods of conservation in 'chemically testing the paint' and filling the bed

Below For Handel, 25 Brook Street was a comfortable home, convenient for both St James' Palace and the Haymarket, where he conducted most of his business. He had it fitted out with a rehearsal and performance room, still in use today.

with 'authentic horse hair and feathers', it might have paid a short visit to Dennis Severs House in Spitalfields (see page 45) to find cheaper paths to authenticity. Next door was Jimi Hendrix's house, offering a glorious challenge in London musical contrast.

Home house

Robert Adam's London showcase, restored to its former glory

20 Portman Square, London W1; private house, open by arrangement

Nowhere in London conveys the splendour of a first-rate Georgian town house as does 20 Portman Square. It is Robert Adam's urban masterpiece. That West London once had dozens of properties of comparable quality, almost all gone, is heart-breaking. The rescue of Home House after its dereliction at the hands of London University's Courtauld Institute of Art was long and painful. It is now a private club, with a big-screen television in the bar and piped pop music in the music room. But the restoration has been immaculate. Open by appointment, Home House is still a London wonder, an echo of the old West End.

The house was begun in 1772 for the widowed Elizabeth, Countess of Home, rich on the Jamaica trade and disreputable with it. Lady Montagu, her neighbour, referred to her as 'Queen of Hell'. The first designs were by James Wyatt but when he became dilatory, his rival, Robert Adam, was summoned. The latter completely overlaid the former's work, eager to outstrip his competitor in every way. Each room is a variation on a Roman theme. The Adam team of Joseph Rose, Angelica Kauffmann and Antonio Zucchi adorned the interiors. With demolished Derby House, this was to be Adam's London showpiece and advertisement.

'It is Robert Adam's **urban masterpiece.'**

Left The restoration of
Robert Adam's stairs was
based on his surviving
drawings for the interiors
of Home House, now in the
Sir John Soane's Museum.
Below A doorway in the
Etruscan Room opens onto
a secret stair leading to a
room above. It was
rumoured that Lady Home
used these stairs when she
'entertained' young male
visitors in the afternoon.

The exterior of London's terrace houses in
the 18th century display their wealth only in the
width of their façades and grandeur of their
doorcases. Home House was erected on a site
five bays wide. This gave Adam three bays for
the reception rooms and a full two for an
entrance hall with a circular stair rising the
height of the building. Though outwardly a
simple brick terrace, the interior has the scale
of a country house turned sideways and slotting
into the square.

The ground floor is of rooms mostly by
Wyatt but redecorated by Adam. They had been
near-wrecked by the Courtauld, with shelves
clambering up the walls and pipes and wiring
everywhere (in an institute dedicated to art!).
All is now well. The front room has its fireplace,
walls and ceiling reunited. Red scagliola columns
fill the corners and lend an illusion of length.

Large doors open to reveal the dining room
to the rear, again showing Adam's genius at
making modest shapes seem grand. An apse is
inserted at one end while enriched pilasters run
from floor almost to ceiling to increase the
impression of height. The ceiling, Adam at his
most effortless, adds width, decorated by
Zucchi's medallions. Beyond is the Countess's
private drawing room, again adorned by the
remarkable Zucchi.

These rooms were for domestic use. Upstairs
is the *piano nobile* reached by one of the finest

staircases in London. From the relative gloom of the lobby, it swirls upwards towards the light. One flight divides into two, then turns back onto the landing, a contained architectural explosion. The walls are adorned with Rose's plaster trophies and Zucchi's grisaille paintings. Above is the rotunda of a miniature pantheon.

At the top of the stairs, the visitor must turn left and enter an ante-room before beginning the formal parade. This room, with a Raeburn over the mantelpiece, was the office of the art historian and spy, Anthony Blunt, when director of the Courtauld.

The music room ceiling teases the eye with circles gently bumping into one another. Here Zucchi's paintings are musical. Adam's fitted organ has been re-created against the side wall, but modern clubroom-style armchairs jar with the decoration.

The adjacent drawing room doors, fireplace and ceiling are Adam originals, richer and more colourful than in the music room. Eileen Harris, in her essay on the house, describes the frieze as of 'laurel arches springing from baskets of anthemia, and standing nymphs supporting *tazze* draped with husk chains'. The ceiling depicts Venus reading the *Aeneid* to Augustus Caesar. The decoration is the epitome of Roman virtue. Can this have been the choice of the 'Queen of Hell'?

We pass through what was Lady Home's dressing room but became a belvedere over the garden, looking over the Marylebone fields to the north. The room is circular, with curved cupboards and fireplace, an hors d'oeuvre to the Etruscan Room beyond. Here, as at Osterley Park (see page 146), Adam displays ancient Roman motifs to 'differ from anything hitherto practised in Europe'. The walls had been destroyed and were reproduced from drawings in the Soane Museum. They drip with fronds, popinjays and grotesques. Here are Zucchi cameos everywhere, delicate on white backgrounds.

Home House was leased by Stephen and Virginia Courtauld in 1926. They not only restored the Adam rooms but created sumptuous bedrooms on the upper floor by the same fashionable Art Deco stylist, Peter Malacrida, they used at Eltham Palace (see page 90). *Country Life* called the resulting style 'Georgian Art Deco Alma Tadema, and sheer smartness'.

The rooms (which can be hired) show a liberal use of marble, black glass, aluminium leaf and ebonized woodwork. The glorious Chinese Room has 18th-century wallpaper and an astonishing Gaudi-esque fireplace. The bathroom is one of the best Art Deco rooms in London.

Above The restoration of the Music Room included copying Adam's original built-in organ. The piece has not been re-created as a musical instrument, however, but as a drinks' cabinet.

Dr Johnson's house

★★ Georgian residence of the great lexicographer

17 Gough Square, London EC4; museum, open all year

Above A portrait of Dr Johnson (1709–84) by Sir Joshua Reynolds, painted in 1775. Johnson compiled his great *Dictionary of the English Language* (published 1755) in the garret room at 17 Gough Square.

No house can properly evoke Samuel Johnson. His personality requires people, conversation, a dinner table, an inn, a clubhouse, not bricks and mortar. It is perhaps as well that Dr Johnson's House does not try. He arrived in London from Lichfield in 1737 and was to live in a variety of rented lodgings round Fleet Street while he tried to support himself by writing. Boswell lists seventeen residences over the course of Johnson's London career.

The house in Gough Square was his home for ten years from 1748, roughly the period of his work on the *Rambler* periodical and the *Dictionary*. The latter's supposed patronage by Lord Chesterfield was meant to pay the rent, but this was not forthcoming. Small wonder he was so rude about Chesterfield's patronage and his letters (see Ranger's House, page 102).

Johnson at this time was perpetually destitute. Visitors were coming and going from the house, his assistants worked for a pittance in the attic and he himself was constantly vanishing to inns, chop houses and clubs. He was as desperate for company as he was for money.

The Gough Square years saw Johnson in his forties, unhappy, overworked and poor. He had not yet won his celebrated pension, nor met his companion, Boswell. It was here that his beloved wife, Tetty, died in 1752, leaving him utterly bereft. In 1759 he moved to smaller and cheaper lodgings in Staple Inn.

After Johnson's departure, the house was sub-let as rooms and became a hotel. It was near derelict in 1911 when Cecil Harmsworth, brother of Lords Northcliffe and Rothermere, bought and restored it. He erected a tiny cottage across the courtyard for a custodian. Although bombed in the war and often on hard times, the house is maintained by the Harmsworth trustees and the City of London.

Above The portrait above the library fireplace at Gough Square is of Elizabeth Carter, a prolific author and outstanding Greek scholar who was one of the 18th-century intellectual women nicknamed 'bluestocking'. Carter was numbered among Johnson's intimate circle of friends and dined often at his London home, alongside other regulars such as Oliver Goldsmith, Edmund Burke and Joshua Reynolds.

The building itself is a conventional William-and-Mary town house, first known to have been owned by a City merchant named Gough in 1700. It is of four storeys with a handsome front door up a flight of steps. Exposed window woodwork predates the anti-fire building acts.

There is little Johnson aura about the interior, compared with his birthplace house in Lichfield, Staffordshire. There, the effigies of his father at his labours and the young Samuel reading *Hamlet* by the kitchen fire are truly moving. Gough Square might be the house of a tidy-minded Fleet Street lawyer.

The basement, where Johnson endured such food as he could afford and drank his eternal cups of tea, displays watercolours. In the parlour are portraits of his associates, including Frank Barber, the negro servant who lived with Johnson after his wife's death, on and off until the end. The childless Johnson made him his heir. Here too stayed Anna Williams, a Welsh poetess and friend of Tetty, whom Johnson also took into his company. Johnson found tea with Anna a constant comfort in adversity.

The rooms on the first and second floors are a museum of Johnsoniana. Even the garret, where the *Dictionary* was compiled, restored after being gutted in the war, might be awaiting a genteel society meeting. The lights are neon.

I long for some of the chaos and clutter of an 18th-century lexicographer's studio, with assistants beavering over the stacks of manuscript slips. 'We extend our knowledge of a person when we look at his home,' wrote Kate Marsh of writers' houses. This one needs more of that 'home'.

1 & 2 Kensington court

⭐ Grand London town houses built for wealthy Victorians

Kensington Road, London W8; now a hotel

Kensington Court was a Restoration mansion lying to the south of Kensington Palace. The old house fell on hard times, became a school then a lunatic asylum and was replaced in the 1880s by a development of the same name. The developer was Jonathan Carr, fresh from building Bedford Park in Chiswick. Here he employed the same Queen Anne Revival but on a denser, more urban plan. The east side of Kensington Court is, in my view, the most handsome group of town houses in London, of dressed red brick and terracotta with white porches and balconies on ornamental brackets. The architect was J. J. Stevenson.

The old house itself was replaced by two houses facing Kensington Gardens, Nos.1 and 2, now forming the Milestone Hotel. The milestone itself is concealed behind the railings. No.1 is by Stevenson, with two Dutch gables and a corner turret. Its owner was Lord Redesdale, the grandfather of the Mitford sisters, who built Batsford Park, in Gloucestershire, in a similar style.

The corner house, No.2, is more eccentric. It is the only London building by the flamboyant Oxford revivalist T. G. Jackson, designer of Hertford College in Oxfordshire. It is in wild Franco-Flemish Gothic coated with early Renaissance motifs and might be nestling beside a canal in Bruges. Tall strip pilasters rise the complete height of the façade. A recessed side entrance is topped by an aggressive balcony. The windows, some with Gothic tracery, have beautifully dressed surrounds. Dolphins cavort above a bold oriel window. The owner was a tycoon called Athelstan Riley whose initials are on the dressings.

The houses became a hotel in the 1920s but fell derelict after a suspicious fire in 1986. Not until 1991 was the hotel restored and reopened. The main entrance lobby had been altered, but the Jackson interiors appear to survive. The sitting room is neo-Jacobean with panelling and an alcove overlooking the park. The dining room is equally so, with heavy Tudor pendants to its ceiling. The main first floor suite claims to be the most sumptuous in any London hotel.

'Kensington is London's **most unobtrusive** royal palace ...'

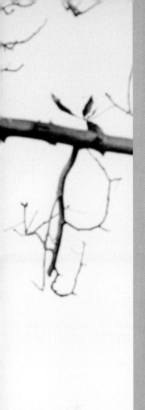

Kensington palace

★★★★☆ Palace extended by Sir Christopher Wren with state rooms painted by William Kent

In Kensington Gardens, London W8; museum, open all year

Kensington is London's most unobtrusive royal palace, yet also its most satisfying. The original house on the site was a comfortable country seat that had appealed to William of Orange, newly arrived from Holland in 1688. He suffered from asthma and his queen, Mary, hated the dampness of Whitehall, 'nothing but water and wall'. They were already rebuilding Hampton Court up river, but needed a place nearer Westminster in the meantime. The Earl of Nottingham's house in Kensington suited them well and was bought in 1689 for £20,000.

The small Jacobean building was speedily extended by Wren, with four pavilions added to the corners of the old house within six months of purchase. The house grew steadily under Wren's assistant, Nicholas Hawksmoor, to its present formlessness. What was left of the old house then vanished completely under George I, with alterations by Colen Campbell and William Kent.

At its peak of popularity under the Hanoverians, Kensington accommodated a Court of 600 people. The Royal Family moved to Buckingham House in 1760 and Kensington later became the residence of the King's son, the Duke of Kent. It was the birthplace of Princess Victoria in 1819. It was she who ordered its rescue from dereliction and opening to the public in 1899.

Part of Kensington is still a residence for 'lesser Royals'. Their apartments include the west range and principal entrance, set round three courtyards not yet on public view. At the time of writing, visitors to the state rooms must make a furtive 'tradesman's entrance' from the north. Since the state rooms cannot be approached as intended, their layout is confusing. Visitors first see a downstairs display of royal costumes, such as a selection of the Queen's hats or a fine array of clothes worn by Diana, Princess of Wales, one-time resident. The adjacent Red Saloon is where the eighteen-year-old Queen Victoria held her first Privy Council on inheriting the throne in 1837.

The pleasure of what is visible at Kensington lies, as at Hampton Court (see page 130), in the contrast between the Anglo-Dutch domesticity of the Royal Family's private quarters and the grandeur of the state rooms. The latter are reached first up the King's Grand Staircase. This is one of the finest in London, of marble and painted by William Kent. Even Horace Walpole, no fan of Kent, admitted it was 'the least defective work of his pencil'.

The space is dominated by a vast *trompe-l'œil* mural filling the upper storey and depicting members of George I's court crowding an arcade overlooking the stairs. Among their number is the 'wild boy' found in the German woods on all fours and widely exhibited as a Court curiosity. The illusion continues in the ceiling, painted to look like a dome beneath which more courtiers gaze down on the unreal crowd below.

There now begins a circuit of reception rooms built by Wren round the White Court. The Presence Chamber has Kent's ceiling of a red cross on a white background. The mantelpiece is of Grinling Gibbons carving, the walls covered with Italian embroideries. Beyond is the Privy Chamber, hung with Mortlake tapestries and filled with busts of English scientists and philosophers. Here Kent's ceiling depicts Mars and Minerva as George I and his Queen, surrounded by the arts and sciences in a state of luxury they rarely enjoy today.

The exquisite Cupola Room is again by Kent, and a dramatic change from his previous chambers. This is of Roman grandeur, fluted pilasters rising to a huge coffered ceiling, painted with *trompe l'œil* to give added height. Round the walls are statues of Roman gods, gilded and in niches. In the centre of the room is one of Kensington's most treasured objects, Roubiliac's clock of the four monarchies of antiquity, Rome, Persia, Macedonia and Chaldea. It once played tunes by Handel and Corelli.

The east range of the circuit begins with the King's Drawing Room, its Kent chimneypiece and ceiling now restored. On a wall is George II's 'fat Venus' by Vasari, with lesser Old Masters from the Royal Collection. The King's suite was converted for Princess Victoria before her accession and has been restored to that period.

It was in the bedroom here that the Princess was awakened to be told of her accession. The rooms seem happy, sunny chambers, with views over Kensington Gardens. Filled with pictures of

Left William Kent spent five years on the painted decoration of Kensington Palace, beginning in 1722 and finishing with the King's Grand Staircase in 1727. **Centre** The King's Gallery was originally built for William III to hang the best paintings in the royal collection. **Right** Designed by Colen Campbell and painted by Kent, the Cupola Room was the principal state room in George I's remodelled palace. It was here that the future Queen Victoria was baptised, in 1819.

the Princess and young Queen, they contrast with the busy mother or gloomy old lady so often depicted later in her reign. These are the rooms of a truly 'Victorian' teenager.

The Queen's rooms were those built earlier, for Mary II, and are quite different. They suggest the domestic interiors of a comfortable house in The Hague. The walls are panelled or papered, the floors are of oak and the furnishings cosy. Fireplaces have been restored with their brick backings. There are many paintings by Kneller and some of the Queen's avidly collected Chinese porcelain.

The Queen's Gallery has a fine barrel-vaulted ceiling and Gibbons's work on the overmantels. Here she would meet with her ladies-in-waiting, sitting with their embroidery whilst being read to beneath portraits of monarchs overhead.

Little of the formal gardens left by Queen Mary and her sister, Queen Anne, survives at Kensington, although we still have Queen Anne's beautifully proportioned Orangery by Hawksmoor. The 18th-century love of naturalism swept them away in favour of lawn. But the parkland of today's Kensington Gardens would doubtless be a housing estate in the manner of Bayswater but for William's urgent need to escape Whitehall. His asthma was London's most lucky circumstance.

Lambeth palace

★ ☆ Archbishop of Canterbury's London home with 17th-century Great Hall

Lambeth Palace Road, London SE1; private house, open part year

Lambeth Palace, the London home of the Archbishops of Canterbury, was until recently closed to the public. Its austere gatehouse and high walls along the Embankment seemed to bespeak archiepiscopal aloofness. The palace might be that of the Church at bay, facing the Crown and Parliament across the river, not to mention the old Abbot of Westminster. It was opened to the public by Archbishop Carey in 2000.

The present residence and offices are to the rear, in a Victorian range by Edward Blore, facing a spacious courtyard and gardens. Blore swept away half of the medieval palace in favour of his own version of medieval, a style reminiscent of an overblown country rectory. The interiors of Blore's palace are institutional but colourful. A sequence of reception rooms runs to the left of the entrance stairs, joining the surviving older building at the end of a long corridor. The latter begins with the rebuilt Guard Room, by Blore but with old roof timbers, and hung with portraits of past archbishops. Beyond are the remains of the palace cloisters.

The oldest surviving buildings are visible along the river. Lambeth's magnificent Great Hall is now the palace library. It was comprehensively restored after severe bomb damage and has a hammerbeam roof to rival Westminster's. This was an architectural curiosity, erected in the 1660s after the Restoration but, like halls in Oxford and

Above The original Great Hall of Lambeth Palace was ransacked by Cromwellian troops during the Civil War. Archbishop William Juxon began rebuilding it in 1660 and the work was completed in 1663 at a cost of some £10,000. The Hall has been used as part of the palace library since 1829.

Cambridge colleges, a deliberate reversion to the Gothic of the 'old religion'. Even so, the exterior carries classical features, including ball finials and a pediment over the oriel windows. Inside, the form of a Gothic hall again 'crosses over' into classical alcoves and doorways.

The other principal room on display is the lovely Early English Chapel. This has lancet windows with Purbeck shafts and ribbed vaults. Severely damaged in the war, it was ferociously repainted in 1988 by Leonard Rosoman in a style I would call Byzantine Primitive. Beneath is a Gothic undercroft.

Leighton house

★★★ Artist and collector's residence with extraordinary interior decor

12 Holland Park Road, London W14; museum, open all year

Leighton House is the 'unique expression of the taste and sensibility of one man', says its guide. The man was Frederic Leighton, aesthete, artist and collector. The house was built in 1864, near that of his friend G. F. Watts, on the Holland Estate, an enclave of artists' houses encouraged by the 'aesthetic' Lady Holland of the adjacent Holland House.

These artists were by no means Bohemian. Leighton had just sold his painting, *Dante in Exile*, for the huge sum of £1,000. He was a wealthy young man whose talent was fuelled by years spent with his parents in Italy and France. His portraiture in the Pre-Raphaelite tradition was accomplished and his social celebrity no less so. He was the only artist of his generation to be made a peer, albeit on his deathbed.

The house, designed by Leighton with George Aitchison, was originally a symmetrical building in red brick. There was a reception room downstairs and a bedroom and large studio upstairs. Leighton did not intend to marry or have guests to stay. This was a house for work and for show. Over the next thirty years, it grew to reflect Leighton's changing taste, especially for Arab art, becoming what he called his 'autobiography'. Now owned by the local council, the impact of Leighton House is diluted by the difficulty such owners have in breathing life into old buildings. Entry is through a shop.

On the ground floor is a sequence of hall, ante-room and Arab Hall, the last being Aitchison's extension of 1877. The Arab Hall was based on the banqueting hall of a Moorish palace in Palermo. A black marble pool with fountain forms the centrepiece, while tiled walls rise to a high dome above. Leighton had friends, including Walter Crane and Randolph Caldecott, design the frieze and column capitals.

The Arab Hall is dominated by Leighton's collection of 16th and 17th-century tiles from the Middle East. They are mostly blue-and-white with arabesques, Arabic script, flowers and exquisite birds, their throats 'slit' so as not to represent 'living creatures'. Looking down from above is a *zenana*, or screened balcony.

The Arab Hall appears to have been entirely for show. Guests would admire it and pass through to the drawing room. This looks out onto the garden, its walls described by Leighton as 'the colour of the tobacco of a good cigar'. Ebony door surrounds imitate picture frames. The same doors appear in the dining room. Both

rooms are hung with pictures by Leighton and his contemporaries, notably Burne-Jones. These shine radiantly from dark wallpaper backgrounds, full of the light and colour of southern Europe.

The staircase has a stuffed peacock perched on a newel post. Upstairs is a smaller hall or Silk Room hung with more paintings. They include Millais' delightful *Shelling Peas*. The biggest room upstairs is Leighton's studio, grandly lit by north facing windows overlooking the garden. It is used for concerts but is still hung with pictures, including Leighton's *Death of Brunelleschi* and *Corinna of Tanagra*. Here too is Burne-Jones's *Uninterpreted Dream*. It cries out for the clutter of an artist's studio.

'The Arab Hall appears to have been entirely for show.'

The stuccoed Italianate exteriors of the
Phillimore Estate in Kensington was old-
fashioned by the time No. 18 was completed in
the 1870s. Its purchaser more than made up for
that. The *Punch* cartoonist, Edward Linley
Sambourne, crammed it with artistic
paraphernalia, which was left untouched by his
son, Roy, and daughter, Maud. The latter's
daughter, the Countess of Rosse, passed the
house in 1989 to Kensington and Chelsea
Council, who display it in tandem with Leighton
House (see previous page). The Victorian
Society was founded here in 1958.

The interior has been restored as the
epitome of late-Victorian 'artistic' taste. In
contrast to Leighton, it is gloriously crammed
with contents of the period. The first impression
is of gloom. This is not Gilbert and Sullivan's

Linley Sambourne house

greenery-yallery but greenery-brownery.
Almost all the walls and ceilings are either early
William Morris or covered in Sambourne's fake
embossed leather patches. Windows are
darkened by stained glass. Carpets are dingy.
Even the lights are covered in shrouds. The
place is deliciously swamped by dark tones.

Yet the house is full of colour. Barely an inch
is without a picture, fabric or display of blue-
and-white china. The Sambournes were not rich
collectors, more Victorian 'car-boot sale' addicts.
Sambourne photographed masterpieces and

Left Linley Sambourne was an avid photographer, joining
the Camera Club in 1893. Many of his photographs,
like this self portrait, were taken in his garden and then
used as an artist's reference for his cartoons.

Above The drawing room occupies all of the first floor. Before he made a top-floor room his studio, Linley worked here in the window; the area was curtained so that his easel and equipment could be easily concealed when visitors came. The Sambournes papered the room with imitation Spanish leather, but left the wall behind pictures bare to save on cost.

framed the prints for his walls. He photographed models and did likewise. Such reproductions coat every room, the frames often fitted like a jigsaw puzzle to leave no wall visible.

Since the rooms survived the 20th century and were regularly photographed, the work of displaying the house as the Sambournes left it has been easy. Downstairs are the dining room and morning room. The first floor is entirely one drawing room, the rear of which was for a time Sambourne's studio. Everywhere are prints,

ceramics, statues and books. Even the bedrooms are as left by the family. Roy Sambourne's bedroom is stacked with signed photographs of actresses whom he escorted, with apparent increasing desperation, in his otherwise indolent youth. He never married but pined over those pictures in solitary old age.

The top floor contains Linley's photographic studio, stacked with nude photographs. This is Victoriana as you will never see it at the V&A but beware of the guided tour.

Lord Chancellor's residence

When the newly appointed Labour Lord Chancellor, Lord Irvine, decided in 1997 to restore his official apartment in the Palace of Westminster there was an explosion of protest. He wanted to install wallpaper and furniture copied from Pugin originals, costing hundreds of thousands of pounds.

Wallpaper ran to £300 a roll. The lights cost £56,000. The Pugin-style oak bed cost £16,000. Nor was the result well received. Pugin never designed these rooms as apartments and critics regarded the reproduction interiors as garish and inappropriate. His lordship wisely responded by opening the apartment. Today, however, the role of the Lord Chancellor is much changed and these rooms are no longer an official residence.

The original Palace of Westminster was among the oldest royal palaces. Its Great Hall was first built by William Rufus and remained throughout the Middle Ages possibly the biggest assembly hall in Europe. Following a great fire in 1834, the palace was rebuilt by Sir Charles Barry and A. W. N. Pugin, only Westminster Hall having survived the conflagration.

The new palace contained only one formal residence, that of the Speaker, a magnificent sequence of state rooms, theoretically to receive the Monarch. These are not open to the public. In 1923 a flat was also fashioned for the Lord Chancellor in a far corner behind Victoria Tower, composed of apartments previously used by Black Rod and the Lords' Librarian.

The apartment comprises a single L-shaped corridor, with bedroom, dining room, sitting room and River Room. The chambers seem heavy and dark in their garb of panelling, curtains and carpets. The wallpapers were made from Pugin's original pearwood blocks and handprinted, as in his day. Age is mellowing the new rather fierce colours, and the furnishings are enlivened by Pugin's mastery of pattern.

Largest and most formal is the River Room with spectacular views up and down the river. The fireplace is of Purbeck marble. Classical marble statues stand ponderously on plinths. The windows contain armorial shields of former Lord Chancellors by Lady Elwyn-Jones, wife of a previous incumbent. The walls are hung with paintings from public collections.

Royal Hospital, Chelsea

'This is London's **best place** to bask in **pure Wren.**'

✷✷ A home for heroes by Sir Christopher Wren

Royal Hospital Road, London SW3; private house, open all year

The Royal Hospital in Chelsea is little known because it is still in use, and will be for as long as there is a British army. In 2001, I attended a reception to celebrate two inmates who had fought at the Battle of the Somme (1916). Visitors may walk through the courts and chat with the veterans on seats against sun-soaked walls. Wren's Great Hall and chapel are open to the public but the wards, now divided into private rooms, are inaccessible.

The hospital was planned by Charles II in emulation of the Hôtel des Invalides in Paris. It was begun in 1682 and the first 476 non-commissioned officers and men moved in seven years later. Despite the grandeur of the plan, along the banks of the Thames, it has none of the ostentation of its Parisian counterpart. After passing it daily

Above A group portrait of Chelsea Pensioners taken in the Royal Hospital Chapel in 1998 to mark the 80th anniversary of the Armistice that ended the First World War.

'At 12 o'clock ... the inmates troop in for lunch.'

Above When the Royal Hospital was built, the Great Hall served as a dining room. The Pensioners sat at 16 tables, one for each ward; each table sat 26 men – two sergeants, two corporals, one drummer and 21 privates. At the end of the 18th century, Pensioners began to take their meals in their quarters, but in 1955 the Hall was reinstated as the dining room.

and hardly noticing it, Carlyle remarked that it was 'quiet, dignified and the work of a gentleman'.

The hospital is still big. It is set round three spacious courtyards, two open to each side and one to the river. The façade to Chelsea is severe, a central portico with attached columns flanked on either side by the high windows of the hall and chapel. Above is a strangely elongated cupola that might have strayed from St Paul's Cathedral. A much finer portico, its columns here detached, adorns the river front. This is London's best place to bask in pure Wren.

The chapel is large, tunnel-vaulted with modest plasterwork. The seats are arranged lengthwise. Over the apsed chancel is a painting by Sebastiano Ricci. The hall is no more decorative, here with a flat ceiling. Not for old soldiers the enrichment that was later to greet old sailors at Greenwich, but at least the soldiers are still here. At 12 o'clock the public is ushered out and the inmates troop in for lunch.

St Barnabas

★ Town house with Rococo plasterwork

Greek Street, London W1; private house, open by arrangement

Most people assume Greek Street has something to do with Greeks. It does not. It was developed in the 1680s by a speculator, Gregory King, who gave the street his name, Greg Street, later altered to Greek. Set on its corner with Soho Square is the House of St Barnabas, built in 1746 and sold to Richard Beckford, brother of the Lord Mayor. In 1861, it became a charitable home for 'distressed ladies'; it was here that Gladstone brought his celebrated vagrant prostitutes to be saved. The house remains the charity's base but is no longer a hostel.

So few ordinary Georgian houses are accessible to public view in London that this example is precious. The house has a calm and stately exterior, its front door marked by two obelisks.

Downstairs are offices but the upstairs rooms are decorated with remarkable Rococo plasterwork. The landing is adorned with bare-breasted women, perhaps fortunate to survive the house's altered purpose. The saloon has the best stucco work, notably round the fireplace.

Two further rooms are less ornate although retaining Rococo ceilings. To look out from here onto the bustle of Soho Square on a summer evening is to imagine a long lost city. Behind the house is a small chapel, designed for the women inmates in 1862.

St John's gate

★ Surviving gatehouse of the ancient headquarters of the Knights Hospitallers

St John's Lane, London EC1; museum, open all year

The old gatehouse is, as they say, steeped in history. Here lived Hogarth's father, who ran a coffee house over the arch. Then it was occupied by Dr Johnson while he worked on the *Gentlemen's Magazine*. Then it became a tavern. Sorely battered in the war, it was none the less restored to its ancient purpose, as the headquarters of the British Order of St John, which succeeded the Knights Hospitallers of St John of Jerusalem. The latter's base was here in Clerkenwell from 1140 until its suppression by Henry VIII. It was later revived as the Order of St John and became much involved in first aid and ambulances.

The original establishment extended across the Clerkenwell Road, with properties covering the area down to Clerkenwell Green. Today, all this has gone, except the chapel and crypt. But the area round the gate was retained and comprehensively rebuilt by the Victorians. It now yields a fine panelled Chapter Hall, built in the medieval manner by Oldrid Scott in 1902, with a Tudor fireplace and much heraldry.

Beyond are two greatly restored Tudor rooms, the Old Chancery and the Council Chamber over the arch. The walls are rich in panelling and portraits of the Order's various royal sponsors. In the Chancery is a display of the Order's silver, once used to serve the food in its hospitals as symbol of the knight's duty 'to serve our Lords, the sick'. The group forms a charming London survival.

Below Mirrors and glazed surfaces in the breakfast room in No. 13 reflect light from the skylights. The 1828 portrait of Soane by Sir Thomas Lawrence hangs in the dining room.

Soane museum

✦✦✦ Quirky home of a scholarly Georgian architect and collector

Lincoln's Inn Fields, London WC2; museum, open all year

This is the most eccentric home in London. An earlier house on the site was rebuilt by the architect, Sir John Soane, for his family and for offices in 1792. Today, it embodies the mania for 'curiosity' collecting that reached a zenith in the late 18th century. The dilettantism of the Grand Tour, focused chiefly on paintings and sculpture, had become obsessive souvenir hunting. Soane was a scholar, fascinated by ruins, beauty, decay, temples and mausoleums. He inhabited them in his mind and re-created them as buildings for any client he could persuade to pay.

Soane rebuilt No. 12 and a year later moved into No. 13, which he also rebuilt as a house and to display his collection. To the conventional Georgian exterior of No. 13, he applied what was originally an open loggia of stone arches, now glazed. These are covered in motifs of Soane's free-style classicism, decorated with caryatids and ornamental brackets from the outside of Westminster Hall.

Soane then bought No. 14, renting out the house but colonizing the yard at the back. By the time of his death in 1837, he had turned the rear of the three properties into a warren of alcoves, passages, light wells and caves. Every inch he crammed with sculptural fragments, with plaster casts, niches, mirrors and display cabinets of objects. Soane was supremely sensitive to architectural drama. There is not a dull corner in the Soane Museum, and certainly not an empty one, except on the upstairs floors which are set aside for study.

A pleasantly scruffy entrance corridor gives onto the main dining room and library. The wall colours here are allegedly based on scraps of paint from a wall in Pompeii. The room is ingeniously framed by giant pendants over its alcoves and is heavy with bookcases. On the wall is a portrait of Soane by Lawrence as an ageing romantic. He was mortified in later life by the refusal of either of his wayward sons, pictured upstairs, to follow in his profession. One devastated him by writing a savage, initially anonymous, critique of his architectural style.

The study and dressing room behind were offices but hardly seem so. They are a classical doodle in three dimensions. Soane wanted students to roam these galleries, sketching and seeking inspiration. Here he arranged his fragments of ancient Rome and fashioned alcoves into light-hearted conceits. He parodied the Gothick revival with a 'Monk's parlour', containing the grave of Fanny, his wife's dog. He designed a crypt, a dome and a catacomb and displayed many carvings salvaged from the old Palace of Westminster.

In the centre of the mausoleum is a giant sarcophagus of Seti I (which should never have left Egypt). This spot, wrote Soane, calls back 'so powerfully the recollections of past times that we almost believe we are conversing with our departed friends who now sleep in their silent tombs'. The artist, Benjamin Haydon, claimed to have emerged from this valhalla 'with an expression of delighted relief at finding ourselves again among the living, and with coffee and cake'.

In the picture gallery hang two Hogarth epics, *The Election* and *The Rake's Progress*, alive with pathos and wit. They are cleverly arranged on a series of sliding and folding doors, quaint but not easy to appreciate. Another gallery displays works by Canaletto.

The two most idiosyncratic Soane interiors are the two breakfast rooms, similar to his interiors at Pitzhanger Manor (see page 150). Both display his characteristic shallow arch and flat-domed ceiling. No. 12 offers a 'starfish' vault and trelliswork pattern, decorated with leaves as if in a garden pergola. The other breakfast room, in No. 13, also has a shallow domed roof. It is offset by concealed light wells, softly decorated in ochre and yellow and shimmering with mirrors. Pictures depict buildings and figures, in classical poses.

The museum has recently bought the whole of No. 14 and intends to expand its displays into that building as well.

'There is not a **dull corner** in the Soane Museum, and certainly not an **empty one** ...'

Spencer house

★★★☆ Palladian palace overlooking St James's park

St James's Place, London SW1; private house, open part year

On 20 December 1755, the 1st Earl Spencer secretly married his childhood sweetheart, Georgiana Poyntz, during his 21st birthday ball at Althorp. He had already inherited both the Sunderland and Marlborough fortunes and was rich beyond dreams. The buckles on his honeymoon shoes, made of clusters of diamonds, were alone valued at £30,000.

Spencer duly planned a new London home. The architect of the exterior was John Vardy, pupil of William Kent, but he was superseded inside by James 'Athenian' Stuart. The interiors are Stuart's great work, the apogee of mid-Georgian taste, a temple to the arts and to the Spencers' youthful love. The family continued to use the house until the 1920s. Unlike most of their aristocratic contemporaries they did not yield to developer greed, although they removed fittings to Althorp and rented the building to a club and various corporate tenants.

In 1985 the house was taken over by Lord Rothschild and magnificently restored. It is not only a rare survivor of a St James's mansion, it is also the finest. Its plan and scale are those of a country mansion, a full seven bays with porticoed centre beaming out over the park. The rooms have been refurnished with paintings and furniture contemporary with its construction.

The house is entered from St James's Place. The pleasure of the interior lies in the delicacy of its decoration and the quality of the furnishings. One passes from a 'Roman' entrance hall, heavy with busts and friezes, to a pleasant morning

Above The Palm Room, sited behind the dining room, was where Earl Spencer and gentlemen guests took their port and cigars after dinner, while the ladies retired upstairs to Lady Spencer's room. Gilded palm trees line the walls and Corinthian columns support a frieze of griffins and candelabra. The room's architect, John Vardy, based his designs on those by John Webb for the King's bedchamber at Greenwich Palace, then thought to have been the work of Inigo Jones.

room and ante-room, with an apse with *trompe-l'œil* ceiling. The library beyond might be that of a comfortable town house, with prints depicting the expansion of the Christian church.

The dining room is more grand. It was redesigned by Henry Holland in 1785, with scagliola columns at either end and a Carrara marble fireplace copied from one at Althorp. The curtains are of 'French mohair cut velvet'. On the walls are three Benjamin Wests on loan from the Royal Collection. Behind is the first of the house's sensations, the Palm Room. This is composed of a wall of giant fronds exploding upwards from gilt-barked trunks, from which Corinthian columns rise like unpeeled bananas. Palms also decorate the domed alcove beyond. Olive green walls drip with gold. It is an astonishing chamber. Palm trees were within the Palladian canon, symbolizing architectural and marital fecundity, but rarely displayed with such bravura.

'The house saves its jewel for last.'

Above Designed and executed by James 'Athenian' Stuart, the Painted Room celebrates the Triumph of Love and the Spencers' marital happiness. Images of marriage are part of the decorative scheme: above the fireplace is a copy of a Roman painting, the *Aldobrandini Wedding*; in the apse is a circular grisaille panel based by Stuart on a relief panel of a Greek wedding he had seen at the Acropolis.

The upstairs is even grander. The Great Room at Spencer House is that of a palace. Its walls are covered in Grand Tour paintings but its most majestic feature is its coved ceiling. This carries large medallions of Bacchus, Apollo and Venus, with coffering from Roman and Greek originals and with Pannini landscapes.

The house saves its jewel for last. James Stuart's Painted Room corresponds to the Palm Room below. It boasts 'one of the most famous 18th-century interiors in England'. The form is of a small rectangle with a large apsidal bow window with a screen of fluted and gilded Corinthian columns. The green walls are covered in painted garlands and fronds, as are the pilasters, friezes, medallions and chimneypieces. By daylight or at night, the decoration seems to shimmer in green and gold. The date of the design is *c*1759 and must qualify as a masterpiece of mid-Georgian design. Architecture has finally shaken off the age of Wren and awaits the arrival of Robert Adam. Here it has no need of him.

The Tower of London

Tower Hill, London EC3; museum, open all year

The Tower of London, like Windsor Castle, is dominated by tourism, but not spoilt by it. Its medieval enclave round Water Lane has been well restored and sits at the foot of the Norman tower. Three of the accessible buildings within the enclave qualify as one-time residences, the White Tower itself, the 13th-century palace built by Henry III and Edward I, and the notorious Bloody Tower.

The White Tower ✫✫

Below A view of the White Tower seen from the south, over the River Thames, with the 13th-century Lanthorn Tower in the foreground.

The scale of William I's keep is impressive, still defying the fortresses of commerce investing it on all sides. This is the largest and most complete Norman castle of its type in England. It was built as a fort and a palace c1078, of ragstone whitewashed in the 13th century, hence the name. A sign of its palatial purpose is both the scale of the main rooms and the presence of a chapel, its apsidal east end pushing out through the keep wall.

Much has changed over the years. Medieval additions have been removed, windows altered and stone replaced. The fussy caps on the corner towers are 17th century. The removal of the surrounding clutter, mostly by the Victorians, has returned the tower to its Norman form. It is now an armoury museum, honouring its use from medieval times as the chief Royal Arsenal. It could do with some corner of its Norman domesticity restored.

The interior is divided down the middle by a huge wall, splitting each of the three floors into two chambers. The ground floor rooms would have belonged originally to the Constable of the Tower and retain their massive ceiling beams, deep window openings and Norman fireplaces. The first floor was the main ceremonial floor, one side acting as a Great Hall and the other as a Great Chamber. This originally rose the full height of the rest of the tower. Garderobes flank the side passages. Here too is the Chapel of St John, a rare unaltered Norman chapel, two-storey and unadorned apart from the carvings of the pier capitals. It was here that Mary I was betrothed 'by proxy' to Philip of Spain in 1554, the most perilous marriage in English history.

The upper storey, which has neither garderobes nor fireplaces, was probably a later insertion, perhaps when the tower was superseded by Henry III's new palace by the river. It housed important political prisoners but was later converted for storage. By Elizabeth I's reign it was an armoury. This, in varying forms, it has been ever since.

The Medieval Palace ✳

The residential buildings erected by Henry III and Edward I in the course of the 13th century were restored in the 1990s to how they were when the Tower was the monarch's chief residence in the City. Overlooking the Thames, they straddle Water Lane in the Inner Ward and comprise Wakefield Tower and St Thomas's Tower above Traitor's Gate. The composition is now more picturesque than grim, especially as previously restored by Antony Salvin in the 1860s.

The 13th-century King's aula, or great hall, has been left 'as found', that is as found by the archaeologists. Wall materials show through and fireplaces have been left ruined. Next door is the King's chamber, properly presented with decorated fireplace hood, painted walls and furniture. A small oratory to one side looks out over the river. On a misty afternoon, this little alcove is my London secret.

A bridge leads to Wakefield Tower, currently displaying turbulent events from the long reign of Henry III. The chapel screen here is a copy, but the effect is suitably grand.

Below The square St Thomas's Tower (on the right) is linked by a bridge to the curving walls of Wakefield Tower (centre). The Bloody Tower sits over the pointed archway on the left.

The Bloody Tower ✶

Tower Green lies to the west of the White Tower amid a casual group of medieval, Tudor and Georgian buildings. The half-timbered Queen's House, and its medieval predecessor the Lieutenant's Lodging, housed distinguished prisoners, usually in some comfort, and may have been where Anne Boleyn and the future Elizabeth I were held. Tower officials had to be careful of their charges, never sure which were to die and which return to power. Guy Fawkes and the Nazi, Rudolf Hess, are among later famous prisoners.

Facing the Green from the southeast corner is the Bloody Tower, which began life in the 1220s, in Henry III's time, as one of the water gates controlling the river entrance to the castle. Its portcullis survives on the ground floor. It was later converted to a land gate and extended as residential lodgings, probably as part of the Constable's quarters. Then known as the Garden Tower, it is traditionally believed to be where the 'Princes in the Tower' were held – the two sons of Edward IV who may or may not have been murdered by Richard III.

The Bloody Tower was heightened to add an extra floor for the occupancy of Sir Walter Raleigh and his family, surely the only death cell to have been so lavishly improved for one inmate. The lower chamber is displayed as during Raleigh's time, a rush-matted study with desk, quill pens and books. Raleigh was imprisoned here in 1603 on a charge of high treason against James I. He finally went to the scaffold in 1618.

Above Raleigh was fairly comfortably lodged in the Bloody Tower, and he wrote his *Historie of the World* while a prisoner there. In 1616, he negotiated a temporary release to lead an expedition to South America in search of the fabled El Dorado. During the expedition Raleigh's men attacked a Spanish outpost and on his return to England the outraged Spanish ambassador insisted that his death sentence be reinstated. Raleigh was executed on 29 October 1618.

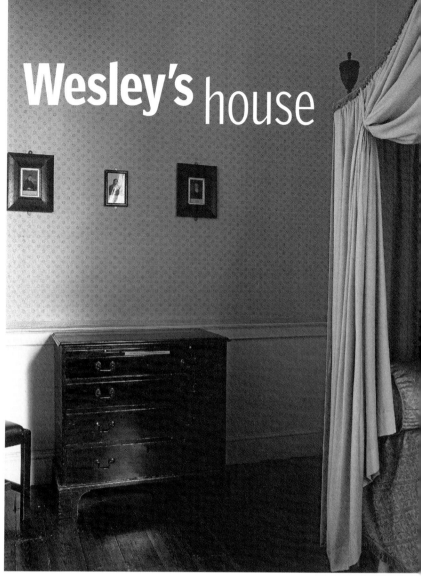

Wesley's house

Right The bedroom where John Wesley died on 2 March 1791. His house was built in 1779 next to the chapel, finished the previous year, that replaced the Methodists' original London base at the Foundery. **Below right** A portrait of Wesley painted in 1765, when he was 62 years old. It now hangs in his study.

✶ ✶   Georgian town house of the celebrated Methodist preacher

47 City Road, London EC1; museum, open all year

John Wesley and his brother Charles set up their first society in the old Foundery on Aldersgate in 1740. Although the Methodists did not split from the Church of England until 1791, they were denied worship in Anglican churches. They held 'meetings' at first in the open air, then in chapels. The Wesleys lived in or near the Foundery premises from the start.

The house is exceptionally simple, although this may be because of the paucity of the present furnishings. The Wesleys were not poor. There is a kitchen and associated offices downstairs. The ground floor drawing room looks out peacefully over a small garden, across the City Road to Bunhill Fields. It is a sylvan moment in central London. Wesley's exercise horse stands by the wall with an electric shock machine for treating his ailments.

Upstairs is the great preacher's study and library, still with his annotated books in the bookcase. Behind is the bedroom and bed in which he died in 1791. A small room beyond was his private prayer room, his Bible open at The Psalms.

Few visitors to Westminster Abbey penetrate to the glories hidden behind. Here in the remains of the old monastery are two cloisters housing Abbey officials and extending to the adjacent buildings occupied by Westminster School. Alleys and cloisters are open to the public and more of pre-Reformation London can be seen in these courts than anywhere else. The enclave is a quiet retreat in the heart of the capital. The Little Cloister is such a favourite that I hesitate even to mention it.

The entrance to the former monastic buildings is either through the Abbey or through Dean's Yard. The East Cloister embraces the great Chapter House, Pyx Chamber and various undercrofts and museums. From here, an ancient and mysterious medieval vaulted passage leads to the Little Cloister, formerly known as Farmery Court, on the site of the old Infirmary. Although damaged in the Second World War and with a 17th-century arched arcade, it retains its medieval aura. Walls, windows and doors seem to have been gathered from all ages. A fountain plays in the middle. On a warm summer day, it might be a courtyard of an almshouse in old Seville.

Westminster Abbey Little cloister

★ ★ Medieval Abbey cloisters

Dean's Yard, London SW1; private residence, can be viewed from public areas of the Abbey

Royal Naval Hospital, Greenwich

East

London East

Charlton house

★★ Jacobean mansion house with ornamental frontispiece

Charlton Road, London SE7; museum, open for groups by arrangement

All my Victorian guidebooks to London assert, in a burst of antiquarian zeal, that 'Inigo Jones was the architect of Charlton'. Sadly, there is no evidence for this, and little likelihood. Today, East London's premier 17th-century mansion (after Greenwich) cuts a sorry spectacle. Birmingham honours its Aston Hall and Leeds its Temple Newsam. Charlton House has been owned by Greenwich council since 1925 and is now a public library, municipal offices and meeting rooms. The grounds are divided into playing fields. The approach is covered in tarmac. Surely Greenwich can do better.

Charlton is an intact E-plan house built for Sir Adam Newton, Dean of Durham and tutor to James I's son, Henry, between 1607 and 1612. The house was bought in the 18th century by the Maryon Wilson family, lords of the manor of Hampstead, but was usually tenanted. Norman Shaw added a wing in 1877. Most of the original ceilings, staircases and fireplaces survive. Restored and refurnished it would be a glorious addition to the sparse attractions of south-east London. Today we can only wander empty rooms and dream.

The exterior of Charlton is tremendous. The main front carries a supremely ornamental frontispiece, the sort of Mannerist Renaissance composition one might find on a merchant's town house in Germany or the Low Countries. Pevsner called it 'the most exuberant and undisciplined ornament in all England'. Paired columns either side of the door rise

of the character suggested by old *Country Life* photographs of the house. The overmantels merit a gallery to themselves. Some are wildly Mannerist, some restrained classical, some black marble, some soft plaster relief. That in the saloon is attributed to Nicholas Stone. These overmantels represent the height of Jacobean taste in early 17th century London. In the black polished surface of one fireplace a former resident is said to have seen reflected a murder being committed on the heath outside.

to niches, consoles and brackets coated with strapwork. The whole front is united by a pierced balustrade. There is nothing like it in London, although the style was to be revived in late-Victorian developments such as Kensington Court (see page 55).

The house has a two-storey Great Hall running from front to back of the building, similar to Hardwick Hall, in Derbyshire. As at Hardwick, the grandest rooms are on the top floor. The staircase is remarkable, rising through three storeys with a different order of balusters on each floor. The supports are extraordinary, carved as palm tree trunks rising from vases. Red Indian headdresses, a favourite motif of the period, peer at us from the gloom. This is most exotic.

The rooms retain a wealth of Jacobean plasterwork but otherwise are without any

Down house

★★ Charles Darwin's family home, preserved as a shrine

Luxted Road, Downe; English Heritage, open part year

Charles Darwin brought his growing family to this Kent village in 1842, six years after returning aboard the *Beagle*. He was to spend fifteen years bringing his *On the Origin of Species* to publication, tortured by doubt over its possible reception. Recurring illness bordering on hypochondria was relieved by wandering the fields behind the house. Not until a colleague was on the brink of publishing ideas similar to his own did he rush his book to print in 1859. He became an instant celebrity. Yet he stayed at Down House until his death, surrounded by his seven surviving children, his fame and contentment.

Charles Darwin
1809–82

Darwin was born in Shrewsbury in 1809. He was studying at Cambridge when, in 1831, he had the opportunity to join an expedition to the Pacific as the naturalist on board HMS *Beagle*. The voyage famously took in the Galapagos Islands and the observations he made there helped him to develop the theories on evolution published in *On the Origin of Species*. In 1839 Darwin married his cousin, Emma Wedgwood, and they moved to Down in 1842, shortly before the birth of their third child. Darwin died there on 19 April 1882 and was buried in Westminster Abbey, close to the tomb of Sir Isaac Newton.

Right It was in the old study at Down House that Darwin wrote his famous book, *On the Origin of Species by Means of Natural Selection, or The Preservation of Favoured Races in the Struggle for Life*, to use its full title. In 1877 the Darwins had the study converted into a smoking room, but it has since been restored to its former purpose.

After Darwin's death, the family moved away and the house was taken over by Downe House, a school for girls (the -e was an affectation). When this moved to bigger premises, it kept the name. Down House was opened as a museum in 1929 under the aegis of the British Association for the Advancement of Science. Not until 1996 was a full restoration undertaken by English Heritage. The first floor is a museum to Darwin's life and work, mostly audio-visual displays. The ground floor has been reinstated as it was in his later years.

Down House lies in a precious fragment of countryside within the boundaries of Greater London. Here woods, fields and villages south of Orpington are so vulnerable that a fingerpost sign is treated as a historic building. The house itself is a conventional Victorian villa set in spacious grounds whose appeal lies chiefly in the ghost of the great man wandering their borders, collecting beetles and leaves and watching the seasons reveal the mysteries of nature.

The heart of the house is the study located in the middle of the ground floor. Darwin enjoyed his children roaming in and out. Here, he said, 'my life goes on like clockwork'. A daughter wrote, 'He always made us feel that we were each of us creatures whose opinions and thoughts were valuable to him, so that whatever there was best in us came out in the sunshine of his presence.'

The room has been re-created as Darwin left it, which means in rather a mess. His wife, Emma, was known as 'Miss Slip-slop'. She had liked the young Darwin for 'not being fastidious' about tidiness. The room is a clutter of rocks, phials, skeletons, notebooks and spiked scraps of paper. Books are scattered everywhere. In one corner a screen hides Darwin's privy.

The other rooms are also disordered. In the drawing room, books are left open on chairs. Croquet mallets litter the hall. Coats hang at random. A Victorian family has gone out for a walk and will be back soon.

Eastbury Manor house

Eastbury Square, Barking; National Trust, open all year

The old manor of Barking Abbey towers over the surrounding bog of semi-detached suburb, as if pleading for rescue. It was built by a City merchant, Clement Sysley, in the 1550s and little altered, though often decayed, since then. Used as a farmhouse, it was close to ruin when, in 1918, the Society for the Protection of Ancient Buildings galloped over the horizon and forced it on the National Trust. Eastbury is now run by Barking's leisure department, well maintained if mostly empty.

The house from the outside is tall and distinguished, retaining a respectable skirt of garden. This is no manorial farm house, as might at first appear, but a serious, three-storeyed mansion. The brick exterior is unusually rich. While the east elevation is symmetrical, the north has its balance interrupted by a porch bay surmounted by a pediment. The roof is finely finished, with deep gables, lofty chimneys and a belvedere turret.

The interior has a Great Hall and Great Chamber upstairs, with parlours in the wings. Few fittings survive apart from some panelling but the Great Chamber contains exceptionally good wall paintings. These depict fishing scenes in ornate *trompe-l'œil* frames. The Long Gallery retains its Tudor fireplace. Eastbury should be refurnished as a major London house of the Tudor age.

Eltham lodge

✫ ✫　Restoration mansion and home to an historic golf club

Court Road, London SE9; private house, open by arrangement

The rear wall of Eltham Lodge is the boundary of the 18th green of the Royal Blackheath Golf Club. This has required shatterproof glass to be installed in its windows. One wonders what happened before its invention. The Royal Blackheath claims to be the oldest club in England, instituted by Scottish golfers travelling south for the coronation of James I in 1603. Having played for centuries on the heath itself, members found driving balls across the main London road increasingly hazardous, and merged with the Eltham Club in 1923. Although private, the club welcomes visitors by appointment, and is proud of its small golf museum.

The house exterior is a gem of Restoration architecture. Eltham Palace and its estate were leased from the Crown by Charles II's banker, Sir John Shaw. He let the palace as a farm and in 1664 commissioned Hugh May to build a new mansion a mile to the east. May had been much influenced by Dutch architecture during his exile under the Commonwealth. Tall windows on ground and first floors rise to bold eaves and a sweeping hipped roof. The present garden front, facing the green, has a beautiful pilastered centrepiece with decorative pediment, a style that was to typify English buildings for the best part of a hundred years.

Chief feature of the interior is a superb staircase. This has heavily sculpted relief panels, much painted, rising to a landing and ceiling with an oval garland. Although the rooms are institutionalized and lack period furniture, they have good original ceilings and fireplaces. Paintings of Royal Blackheath officials in traditional red coats take the place of ancestral portraits on the walls.

Eltham palace

★★★★ 'Wrennaissance' style mansion with Art Deco interiors built on medieval ruins

Court Yard, London SE9; English Heritage, open part year

The Eltham mansion of Stephen Courtauld and his wife, Virginia, contains the epitome of lavish inter-war Art Deco. Designed by a talented Italian playboy, Peter Malacrida, it had exotic blackbeam veneers, gold-plated taps and bathrooms smelling of gardenia. There was piped music and a telephone exchange. Virginia had a snake tattooed on her ankle. Stephen owned a rare Burney Streamline car. A pet lemur, Mah-Jongg, enjoyed a cage with bamboo murals and a ladder to help it to bed, all of which was featured in *Country Life*. The glorious dazzle ended with a bang in 1944 when the Courtaulds emigrated to Rhodesia and the house passed to the Army Education Corps.

The restoration of Eltham by English Heritage in 1999 reinstated what is now the finest Art Deco interior in England. The house

was based on an important medieval palace, its Great Hall built by Edward IV at the end of the 15th century. By the early 17th century, it was decaying and from the 18th onwards the palace ruins were solely of antiquarian interest. Jeffry Wyatville in 1827 wanted to demolish the roof and re-erect it at Windsor Castle (see page 26) where it would have been lost in the 1992 fire. Eventually the Office of Works took over and repaired the hall, but an offer from the Courtaulds in 1933 came as a blessing. They wanted a house near London but sufficiently far, they hoped, to be free of suburbs.

Having taken a lease from the Crown, the Courtaulds had to fight objections to building over the ruins. Yet the architects, Seely & Paget, were respectful of the site. The Great Hall was restored as 'Hollywood medieval', with

'This is interior decoration as theatrical performance.'

tapestries, antique furniture and an inserted gallery for minstrels. Next to the hall are two new ranges in a self-consciously 'Wrennaissance' style, above a landscaped moat and sunken garden. (*The Times* was unimpressed, calling the place 'an unfortunately sited cigarette factory'.)

Inside, Seely & Paget went for Art Deco. Money was clearly no object. The entrance hall might be the foyer of an inter-war liner, with a marquetry mural of a Viking and a Roman warrior and scenes from European cities. Stairs with blackbeam veneer sweep up to bizarre portholes round the gallery.

Everything in the house was intended to be 'the latest'. The hall has a coin-box telephone. Fixtures in the walls link hoses to a central vacuum cleaner. Themes from art and literature abound in the reception room decoration. Since the Courtauld collection of paintings was later dispersed (now mostly in Somerset House), English Heritage boldly decided to copy some of them. This works.

Upstairs, Stephen Courtauld's rooms are relatively modest, the wallpaper from Sandersons depicting Kew Gardens. His wife's suite by Malacrida is sumptuous, similar to those he designed for their Art Deco suites at Home House (see page 50). Pilasters are of sycamore on maple 'flexwood' walls. Art Deco fabric covers the chairs and Brueghel copies hang on curved walls.

The principal guest bedroom is decorated with yellow Venetian panelling and fake books. The remaining rooms are in conventional 'Moderne' style. The dining room overlooking the gardens has doors inlaid with exotic animals and excellent copies of missing furnishings. Eltham conveys a sense of English design at its zenith of self-confidence. Nothing since achieved such novelty or conveys such pleasure. This is interior decoration as theatrical performance.

Forty hall

★★ Jacobean mansion with a rare classical façade

Forty Hill, Enfield; museum, open all year

The house sits on the fringe of the metropolis, where Enfield marches with Hertfordshire and rich men's houses were once two a penny. Nearby the 17th-century New River began its refreshing course from Hertfordshire to Islington and down to the taps of London. Forty Hall was begun in 1629 for London merchant and Lord Mayor, Sir Nicholas Raynton. It passed through many families, the last being the Parker Bowles, who sold the house to Enfield Council in 1951.

The house is architecturally odd. The outside appears to be early 17th century, with no basement but with ground and first floors of equal height below a boldly hipped roof. Although much of this façade is of a later date, it is regarded by experts as a rare classical front of the 1620s, and customarily attributed to Inigo Jones. Giles Worsley, historian of English classicism, remarks that 'it is hard to believe there was no link with Jones and it may be that he provided guidance for the architect'.

No less extraordinary is the floor plan. Inside was a traditional layout of screens passage with Great Hall to the left and steward's offices to the right. It is as if Raynton wished to display novelty outside but antiquity within.

All this must now be set aside, since a new entrance hall was inserted in the 18th century, small but astonishingly rich in plasterwork. A pillared screen, perhaps needed to support the upper floor, is meticulously decorated. The walls carry beautiful panels of musical instruments and acting masks.

The earlier screen to the Great Hall is cruder. On the inside, facing the hall, it has chunky pilasters, grotesques and a giant scallop over the door. The walls are panelled and the ceiling is a mass of geometrical scrolls, all traditional Jacobean.

The rest of Forty Hall suffers acute museumitis, with a rash of harsh lighting, lino and council art. The guidebook has the effrontery to dismiss the foliage round the Raynton Room fireplace as 'undistinguished'. Original ceilings and fireplaces survive throughout the house, needing only the touch of a wand to bring them alive. A glorious cedar of Lebanon in the grounds patiently awaits the day.

Flamsteed house

★★ Sir Christopher Wren's house for the Astronomer Royal

Greenwich Park, London SE10; museum, open all year

When Charles II asked the astronomer, John Flamsteed, for his opinion on how to calculate longitude, the great man, in true scholarly fashion, said the question needed more research. The King duly ordered an Observatory on the site of the old fort on the hill behind Greenwich Palace. It should, he said, cost no more than £500. It cost £520. Flamsteed took up residence in 1676 on an 'incompetent allowance' of £100 a year, from which he had to pay his 'surly, silly' assistant. From here he waged continual war on his rival, Sir Isaac Newton, calling him a robber, thief and puppy at meetings of the Royal Society.

Wren was the designer of this cheap operation and the plan could hardly have been more ascetic. It comprised a basement storehouse, four living rooms for Flamsteed and his family above and the Octagon Room for the telescopes on top. Wren described it as 'for the Observator's habitation and a little for Pompe'. Its style was in part that of the old fort, like a sham castle. Wren even built turrets on the roof. Windows are dressed with wood to look like stone.

Given that this is Britain's precursor of the Houston Space Center, its survival is remarkable. The old house is surrounded by the later Observatory complex, extended as larger telescopes arrived.

Below The Octagon Room remains much as it was in Flamsteed's day, with furniture and astronomical instruments of the period. Flamsteed had to provide his own scientific equipment and household goods, so on his death, in 1719, his widow claimed them as personal property, despite a threatened law suit by the Office of Ordnance. Flamsteed's successor as Astronomer Royal was Edmond Halley.

'The building is **picturesquely sited atop** the Greenwich **slope.**'

These are still used for education and exhibition, one containing the famous 'line' across which visitors are able to stand in two hemispheres at once. Pollution has long since driven the astronomers to purer skies elsewhere.

The building is picturesquely sited atop the Greenwich slope. On the roof is still the red ball, raised at 12.55 pm and dropped at 1.00 pm, enabling shipmasters in the Docks to set their chronometers before setting sail. It now signals lunchtime to office workers in Canary Wharf to the north. The old house has been kept as in Flamsteed's day. The downstairs rooms were the official residence of the Astronomer Royal until 1948. They are restored as the chambers of a 17th-century man of letters, with high-backed chairs, dressers, canopied bed and quill pen.

The Octagon Room is a delightful chamber, built high to house the elongated telescopes required by the lenses of the day. The wall panelling is original, as are most of the telescopes and Tompion clocks. Gazing down on the scene are portraits of the early patrons, Charles II and James II. East London is spread out below.

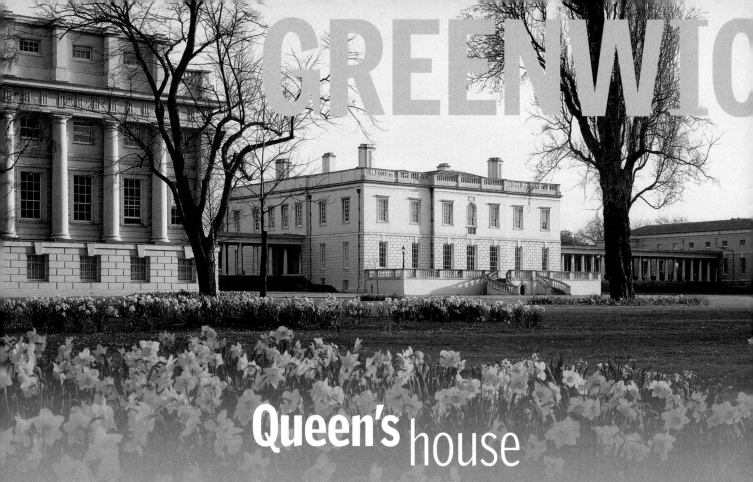

Queen's house

★★★ England's first Palladian house, designed by Inigo Jones

Greenwich Park, London SE10; museum, open all year

Greenwich is one of the set pieces of English architecture, best appreciated from the Isle of Dogs opposite. The scene is dominated by Wren's pavilions (see page 98), rising on their great colonnades as if in homage to the delicate Queen's House sandwiched between and behind them. This house, England's first Palladian building, lies against the steep green of Greenwich Park, with Wren's Observatory (see page 94) set cheekily at an angle on the hill.

The queen was Anne of Denmark, much-tried consort of James I. The house was designed by Inigo Jones on his return from his second visit to Italy, inspired by the light and poise of the south. His villa on the hillside behind the old Tudor palace was to be a dazzling cosmopolitan contrast to the dark and dingy brick palace below. The house was begun in 1616 but unfinished on Anne's death three years later.

Work resumed for Charles I's queen, Henrietta Maria, but still proceeded slowly.

The royal couple were able to use it for just four years before the Civil War. They spent their last night together here in February 1642, Henrietta leaving for the Continent and the King for the battlefields. The King never returned. The Queen visited Greenwich in 1662 after the Restoration, but by then the old palace by the river was being demolished and the site must have been sad.

The building's exterior, displaying Palladio's precise geometry, is unadorned to the point of severity. 'Ye outward ornaments,' wrote Jones, 'ought to be sollid, proporsionable according to the rulles, masculine and unaffected.' A contemporary account called it 'so finished and furnished that it far surpasseth all others of that kind in England'. In the middle of the north façade are two curving flights of steps, a final Baroque flourish. The steps appear from a distance like two tears running down the face of Stuart England.

Jones's original house was in two separate halves, one either side of the old Dover Road which was crossed with small bridges. A loggia at the back was for looking out over Greenwich Park. These bridges were later replaced with east and west ranges completing a building square in plan. If the exterior is chaste, the interior contains the most exquisite Italian and French decoration. The main hall, or Cube Room, must have seemed sensational to visitors used to dark Jacobean halls. The stone floor, by Nicholas Stone, swirls outwards in restless *trompe-l'œil*. To one side rises the cantilevered Tulip Staircase, decorated with a balustrade whose pattern reflected the 17th century's love of these flowers. The stairs enclose what Jones called 'ye vacuum in ye middell', yielding the same giddy effect as Stone's floor pattern below.

Upstairs are a series of sumptuous reception rooms, recently restored and hung with some of the best of the Maritime Museum's admirable picture collection. There are portraits of early Stuarts by Lely, Hogarth, Reynolds and Canaletto. Doors and mantelpieces are decorated with the motifs that crammed Jones's Italian notebooks. Above one door is a theatrical mask, reminding us that architecture is at least in part a show.

Below The Tulip Staircase was the first geometric self-supporting staircase to be built in England. It was modelled on designs by Palladio, who had created the first stairs of this kind at the convent of the Carità in Venice, *c*1560. The Queen's House staircase was finished with a continuous wrought-iron balustrade, decorated with scrolls, leaves and tulip flowers.

GREENWICH
Royal Naval hospital

✦ ✦ Christopher Wren's palatial home for retired mariners

Greenwich Park, London SE10; museum, open all year

The Tudor palace of Placentia was a favourite of Henry VIII. Perhaps for that reason it was not a favourite of his daughter, Elizabeth I. It recovered some life when James I planned the Queen's House in its grounds, designed by Inigo Jones, but soon relapsed as a naval biscuit factory under Cromwell. Greenwich's revival had to await the demolition of the old palace and Charles II's ambition for a rival to Versailles at the seaward gateway to London.

The foundation stone for Charles's palace was laid in 1664 with John Webb, Inigo Jones's pupil, as architect. It was to take the form of three ranges enclosing a square open to the river. The Queen's House would thus have been left obscured, a mere garden villa. Only one range, the western arm, was finished at Charles's death. With the advent of William and Mary, the palace project was converted into one for a naval hospital, with Hawksmoor designing the eastern block to balance that by Webb.

Christopher Wren next put forward plans to replace the proposed third central range with twin pavilions and domes framing the view of the Queen's House behind. This re-casting of Webb's Palladianism as English Baroque has long been controversial. Was it a masterstroke, to keep open the view of Jones's house, or a bruising insult to the original concept? The answer is probably both.

Wren's domes are set on rotundas above colonnades. Each hides the entrance to the two great chambers of the hospital, the Painted Hall to the west and chapel to the east. Beyond stretch Wren's own buildings, the Queen Mary and King William courts, in dazzling Portland stone. The first pensioners arrived in in 1705.

After seeing service as the navy's answer to Wren's Chelsea Hospital, Greenwich became in 1873 the home of the Royal Naval College. It is now Greenwich University and Trinity College of Music. Little remains of its palatial character apart from the Painted Hall and chapel, both open to the public. There are also plans to display some of the old wards for public view.

The Painted Hall is one of England's great chambers. It is in three parts, rising towards the upper hall under arches and gilded pilasters, the ceilings dripping with portrayals of the achievements of William and Mary, Queen Anne and George I. Whatever the politico-religious significance of the Glorious Revolution of 1688, it in no way dimmed the enthusiasm of Stuart and Hanoverian monarchs for depicting their supposed place among the gods on high.

The paintings are by Sir James Thornhill and are his masterpiece. The main ceiling depicts William and Mary, with Louis XIV of France shown as Arbitrary Power, crouching at their feet. The upper hall celebrates the Protestant succession, with William and then George I landing on British soil to keep the wayward British on the path of Reformation virtue. Astronomers describe eclipses. Rivers offer up treasures. Everywhere are symbols of maritime might, reminding English sailors of their deserved glory.

The chapel is restrained in comparison, largely because the original was burned in 1779 and replaced by James 'Athenian' Stuart in the style now associated with Robert Adam. The tiled floor is patterned on ships' cables. The ceiling is that of a drawing room, with *trompe-l'œil* domes and panels filled with leaves. Above the altar is Benjamin West's *Shipwreck of St Paul*. It was here that the survivors of Trafalgar came to give thanks.

Right Sir James Thornhill placed William and Mary at the centre of his magnificent ceiling in the Painted Hall. He began work on the Hall in 1708 at a fee per square yard of £1 for the walls and £3 for the ceiling. It took him 19 years to complete the task. Originally intended as a dining hall for the Greenwich Pensioners, the Painted Hall soon proved too small and was not used again as a naval mess until 1939.

Hall place

⭐ Medieval mansion house with a Restoration extension

Bourne Road, Bexley; museum, open all year

Nestling beneath a roundabout off the noisy A2 appears a mirage. A flint mansion, apparently medieval, sits in a yew garden by a stream. Although overwhelmed by an adjacent leisure centre, Hall Place is real, desperate for a more sensitive reincarnation than as a local art centre.

The house was typical of many in the London suburbs. It was built *c*1537 by a City merchant and Lord Mayor, Sir John Champneys, and consisted of a Great Hall with wings, built of grey-and-white stone and flint in a chequerboard pattern. The hall façade was later altered to make it symmetrical, with a central doorway and a second bay window to balance the original one.

This house was sold in 1649 to another City merchant, Robert Austen, who built a jolly Restoration courtyard onto the back of the old house. This has a pitched roof, redbrick walls and plentiful windows. The join between the old and new house is uncompromising, marked on the garden side by a garderobe tower. The inner courtyard once had open arcades.

After occupation by the Dashwoods of West Wycombe and use as a boys' school, Hall Place was acquired in the early 20th century by the Countess of Limerick. Having lost her children in the Great War she discarded her husband and lived in the house with a lady companion until her death in 1943. She was a considerable bulwark of Bromley society, but the house, which passed to the local council at her death, sadly shows no trace of her occupation. The interior is thoroughly municipalized, the floors aggressively ramped. A smell of school food pervades the place.

What can be seen is the coved ceiling of the Great Hall, with carved bosses and an organ. In the former solar wing is a parlour and Great Chamber. The former has an excellent ceiling with enriched plasterwork, wreaths and fantastic creatures. The gallery above has a barrel vault with more plasterwork and pretty classical window surrounds.

The grounds include a sunken garden, a herb garden and a set of topiary animals.

Right Some of the exterior Tudor flint-and-stone walls at Hall Place were constructed in a distinctive chequerboard pattern. Flint was often used in this decorative way; the dark and shiny surface of knapped flint contrasts well with a lighter coloured stone or brick.

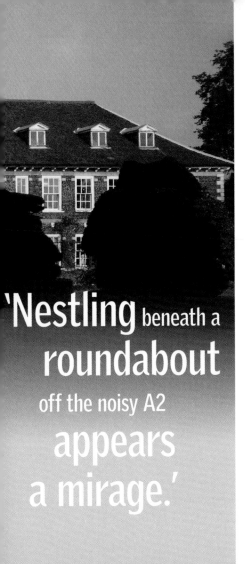

Rainham hall

☆ ☆ Georgian merchant's house with original panelling

The Broadway, Rainham; National Trust, open part year

The hall stands beside a churchyard overlooking bleak Rainham Marshes. These downriver reaches were used to unload heavy cargoes to avoid the journey upstream. Captain John Harle dredged the Ingrebourne inlet and built a wharf to receive coal, marble, timber and Delft tiles. On the proceeds, he built himself this house and a small garden, now owned by the National Trust. They are an adornment of London's otherwise dreary eastern flank.

The house was completed in 1729 in a style still reminiscent of Queen Anne. It is remarkably big, of three storeys with an attic, each storey with arched windows. The front door has a lovely curved canopy with a scrolly pediment. The interior was given a facelift in the 1960s, with fake marble and a touch of Baroque added to the entrance hall. The main reception rooms, still in family use, retain their original panelling and fireplaces. They were clearly fitted out with the products of Harle's business in marble, wood and tiles.

The staircase is excellent. Its original *trompe-l'œil* paintings on either side of the oak leaf swags have been restored. The balusters are of mahogany. I cannot bear to think how many dozens of such houses must have vanished from East London over the past century.

'Nestling beneath a **roundabout** off the noisy A2 appears a mirage.'

101

Ranger's house

★ ★ ☆ William-and-Mary house with added bowed Georgian wings

Chesterfield Walk, London SE10; English Heritage, open all year

Ranger's House was built by an admiral, Francis Hosier, on the hill behind Greenwich, from where he planned to watch ships on the river and dream of the sea. He died in 1727 in the West Indies before he could enjoy this idyll. The house passed to another dreamer, Lord Chesterfield, politician, wit and writer of Polonius-like letters to his illegitimate son, Philip.

Chesterfield's letters were on every topic from politics to food, wine, women, art and table manners. When published, they became hugely popular, although derided by Dr Johnson as 'teaching the morals of a whore and the manners of a dancing master'. In his defence, Chesterfield protested that he merely wanted his illegitimate boy, who would have no place in society, to be 'as near perfection as possible'.

At the time of Chesterfield's occupation, the Hanoverian court was moving upstream to Richmond. He admitted 'that I like the country up, much better than down, the river' and Blackheath was so dangerous that he had to keep a mastiff for protection. Yet he adored the house, spending his summers here from 1748 to 1773 and erecting the present gallery for his art collection. On his death the house passed to a rakish cousin, who married 'beneath him and in secret'. He sold

Above The Long Gallery is home to Bergonzoli's statue of *Cupid and Psyche* (centre), just one item in the vast collection donated by Sir Julius Wernher and now on show at Ranger's House. Sir Julius made his fortune mining for gold and diamonds in South Africa and he used much of it acquiring some of the finest works that money could buy.

Chesterfield's pictures and then his lease to pay his drinking debts. The house passed to the Crown and was used to house junior members of the Royal Family throughout the 19th century.

The house was purchased by London County Council in 1902, for sporting facilities and a teashop. Its fate was transformed in 1974 when the Suffolk family gave the LCC the family collection of Jacobean portraits from Charlton Park in Wiltshire. The house was restored by English Heritage and further enhanced with another donation, of some 600 works of art from the Luton Hoo collection of the South African mining magnate, Sir Julius Wernher. The Suffolk pictures have been moved to Kenwood, and Ranger's House has now surpassed its former opulence.

The house exterior is clearly a marriage of a William-and-Mary centre with Georgian wings. Inside, the downstairs rooms have been decorated to reflect those of the Wernhers' Bath House in Mayfair. The Pink Room has French furniture and porcelain, and Reynolds's portrait of Mrs Uvedale Price. The gallery is hung with Beauvais tapestries and displays one of London's most erotic statues, Bergonzoli's *Cupid and Psyche*. Objects are arranged, for the most part, as in Bath House.

Upstairs is an exhibition of Wernher's promiscuous collecting mania, in the style of the Rothschilds of Waddesdon Manor, in Buckinghamshire. He specialized in the French and Italian Renaissance, especially miniatures and jewellery. There are works by Memling and Filippino Lippi, Renaissance clasps and pendants, Limoges enamels, medieval icons, devotional sculpture and exquisite carved ivory. It is one of London's richest small galleries, woefully under-visited.

Red house

★★★ William Morris's first family home, designed by Philip Webb

Upton Road, Bexleyheath; National Trust, open part year

The arrival of Red House in the National Trust portfolio in 2003 was just cause for celebration. It was designed by Philip Webb in 1859 for the young William Morris and his new wife, Janey. It was to be an enchanted medieval residence, 'a poem of a house', for a community of like-minded artists in orchards well away from the city.

The Morrises lived here for just five happy years, from 1860 to 1865. Like the Wordsworths' Dove Cottage (Cumbria), Red House was the architectural embodiment of an aesthetic ideal. Webb was obsessed with brick, an 'honest' material to challenge the pseudo-stone of stucco London. In Morris's words, Red House would be 'a joyful nook of heaven in an unheavenly world'.

The L-shaped building betrays few of the later Arts and Crafts features associated with the

Morris group. It is closer to the ecclesiastical tradition of Webb's mentors, Butterfield, Street and Pugin. It is more a vicarage than a 'palace of art', and a surprisingly small one. The hipped roof is pitched and tiled, with precipitous gables and lancet windows. The porch has a Gothic arch. The material is red brick, hence the name.

The house was to be decorated by Morris and his friends, Burne-Jones, Madox Brown, Rossetti and Webb, an intention only partly realized. The windows are not generous, but Webb provided abundant light over the stairs and in the studio. The staircase is in simple wood with panelled balusters and newel posts, like those of a Puritan chapel, yet flanked by richly patterned tiles. In the roof above is a glorious stencilled lantern. The upper walls were planned to be covered with murals

Right The functional drawing-room settle was designed by Morris; the ladder and galleried area above were a later addition by Webb. **Bottom** In the light and airy studio, the Morrises kept the walls plain but decorated the ceiling with a geometric pattern of their own design.

depicting the *Siege of Troy*, a strange theme for a Kentish village. These were not executed.

In the first-floor drawing room are unfinished murals by Burne-Jones, based on a medieval romance, that include Morris as the knight with Janey in a wimple. Here is Morris's vast eccentric settle, brought from his studio in Red Lion Square and crowned by Webb with a parapet and stairs that lead to a diminutive minstrels' gallery. The large brick fireplace is self-consciously medieval. The ceiling has a barrel vault.

Most of the furniture is by Webb. Rubbed-brick fireplaces carry medieval mottos, such as 'Our content is our best having' and 'Ars Longa Vita Brevis'. Morris's own motto, 'If I can', was stitched by Janey into embroidery, which it was hoped might cover the walls of the house (but never did). The garden, where no tree was to be chopped down, yielded the plants that inspired the early fabrics. Morris's Daisy pattern became a favourite for girls' rooms into the 20th century. The interior of Red House was later raided for Kelmscott Manor and other Morris museums and private collections, but sufficient remains to evoke the spirit of the place. The house is like the Bloomsbury Set's Charleston, in Sussex, embodying the collective inspiration of young artists in their prime. It was always crowded with friends playing practical jokes on the corpulent Morris, engaging in apple fights, musical evenings and long drives in the country. Webb even designed the wagon that would be sent to greet them from the station.

It did not last. By 1865, Morris's business was flourishing in Red Lion Square but his private income was waning and he hated commuting. He moved Janey and their two girls to London and never returned to Red House. Marital bliss faded and Janey briefly set up home with Rossetti at Kelmscott. No more glad, confident Bexley mornings again.

Sutton house

In Tudor times Sutton House was known as Bryk Place and some original fittings from the period have survived. Much of the carved wood in the linenfold parlour (below) dates from this time; National Trust craftsmen created replicas to replace any missing panels.

Here lies the ghost of old Hackney village. The house was a suburban mansion dating from the 1530s, built by a courtier of Henry VIII, Sir Ralph Sadleir. The substantial three-storey building was gabled, with a Great Hall, mullioned windows and diaper brickwork. What a battering it has taken since then.

Sutton House, named after a later Jacobean owner, was altered in the 18th century, when the Great Hall was divided and the staircase moved. Owners and tenants came and went, including a school, a trade union and a squat. The house passed to the National Trust in 1938 but was scandalously allowed to fall into dereliction. Only in 1990 was it restored and reopened as a local 'resource centre'.

The National Trust could rescue Sutton House's body but not its soul. Linenfold has been restored in the parlour and is some of the finest to be found in London, divided by handsome fluted pilasters. Fragments of 17th-century painting survive on the upstairs walls and more panelling has been restored in the Little and Great Chambers. But shorn of furniture or pictures and filled with municipal chairs, the rooms are lacking in atmosphere. Some effort in this direction is made in the Victorian study and Georgian parlour beyond the Great Chamber.

Everything else is fighting the twin gods of exhibition and education. The most charming part of Sutton House is the Tudor courtyard to the rear, with an arcade and view of the Edwardian 'barn' beyond.

Valence house

⭐ A moated manor house set in the midst of the Becontree Estate

Becontree Avenue, Dagenham; museum, open all year

Some old manor houses still cling to the wreckage in the ocean of estates that covers eastern London. This part of Essex was acquired by the London County Council in the 1920s for 'homes fit for heroes'. Becontree was to become the largest council estate in England, possibly in the world at that time. On a monotonous circular plan, its terraces and cottages spread as far as any eye could see. Privatization has led owners to reface their premises with pebbledash, neo-Tudor or neo-Georgian, depriving them even of their historical curiosity. I wonder if working-class Becontree will ever be as valued as now is working-class Islington.

Even the LCC did not have the nerve to demolish the moated manor of Valence itself. The house had been owned in the 13th century by Agnes de Valence. Although 15th-century fragments remain, this is essentially a 17th-century building. Two sides of the moat survive. Subsequent use as council offices and library has spoiled the environs but the old whitewashed walls survive, with hipped roofs and dormer windows. Here Thomas May, formerly a Devon farmer, raised a stud of horses that were requisitioned for use in the Great War. The Mays lived here until the 1920s.

Downstairs is the old dining room, now with portraits left to the borough by Captain Fanshaw RN in 1963. They are a remarkable find, works by Lely, Kneller, Dobson and Gheeraerts crowded

into a suddenly welcoming, warm panelled room. A rear parlour depicts a Victorian maid preparing a meal. The original staircase, with barley-sugar balusters, leads to another panelled room upstairs. Its period furniture includes a baby's cradle and spinning wheel.

Elsewhere is an exhibition on the development of the Becontree Estate and other memorabilia of Dagenham's history. One room displays the fittings of a 1940s council house. A herb garden has been re-created in the grounds.

Vestry house

★ Georgian house at the heart of a hidden London 'village'

Vestry Road, Walthamstow, London E17; museum, open all year

Church End is a London secret, a village centre lost amid the railway cuttings and terraced grids of late-Victorian Walthamstow. Here is a church, medieval house, almshouses, school and cluster of cottages on the side of a hill towards Epping Forest. In its midst is a bizarre Ionic capital, brought from the demolished General Post Office in the City of London and deposited on the green.

Next to it is a Georgian building of dark brick with white windows. Erected in 1730, it has served in its time as the old workhouse, watch house and vestry meeting room. A 'cage' for keeping troublesome prisoners overnight was added to the outside of the building in 1765. A later use was as a volunteers' exercise hall and armoury. In other words, this building, with its adjacent school and almshouse, was a complete 'one-stop shop' welfare state.

As the population grew and bureaucracy centralized, these functions were all found separate buildings elsewhere. A poorhouse was built. The Metropolitan Police stayed until 1870, installing two prison cells, one of which survives. By the 1880s, even these shreds of local government had departed the village, leaving only a literary and scientific institute and, finally, private tenants. Eventually, in the 1930s, the house became a museum.

Inside, the police cell is still in place and the former armoury has been furnished with panelling and a fireplace from a demolished local manor, Essex Hall. Upstairs are the usual reconstructed rooms of local history. To the rear is a vegetable and fruit garden cultivated by the paupers for their own consumption.

William Morris house

William Morris, who lived here as a boy, wrote of this corner of Walthamstow, 'Hark, the wind in the elm boughs! From London it bloweth/ And telling of gold and of hope and unrest.' He later deplored what had become of the Walthamstow of his youth, 'terribly cockneyfied'. Just as his banker father's speculations had fuelled Morris's socialism, so his witness of the suburbanization of London's environs fuelled his conservationism.

Morris's mother moved to the house in Walthamstow called Water House with her family in 1847 after the unexpected death of her husband at the age of fifty. Morris was thirteen at the time. The family had lived in considerable style in Woodford Hall near Epping Forest, and the move was downhill in every sense.

That said, Water House is hardly modest. It is a big Georgian mansion of 1762 and William himself was left with a legacy sufficient to see him through Oxford and into marriage and business. The façade has two large bows flanking a three-bay centre with classical doorway up a flight of steps. Behind was a large garden with a lake in which the Morris boys fished.

The interior has a large hall running from front to back, where a spacious staircase rises to a no less spacious landing. Here the young Morris would sit for hours, reading or gazing into the garden. The rest of the house is now a gallery filled with a collection of paintings and other works by Burne-Jones, Rossetti, Alma-Tadema and others.

The house would benefit from more of a sense of the domestic. This was, after all, where Morris wrote, 'One looks up and down the field ... and I can't help thinking of tales going on among it all, and long so much for more and more books.' It needs more books.

London

Hampton Court

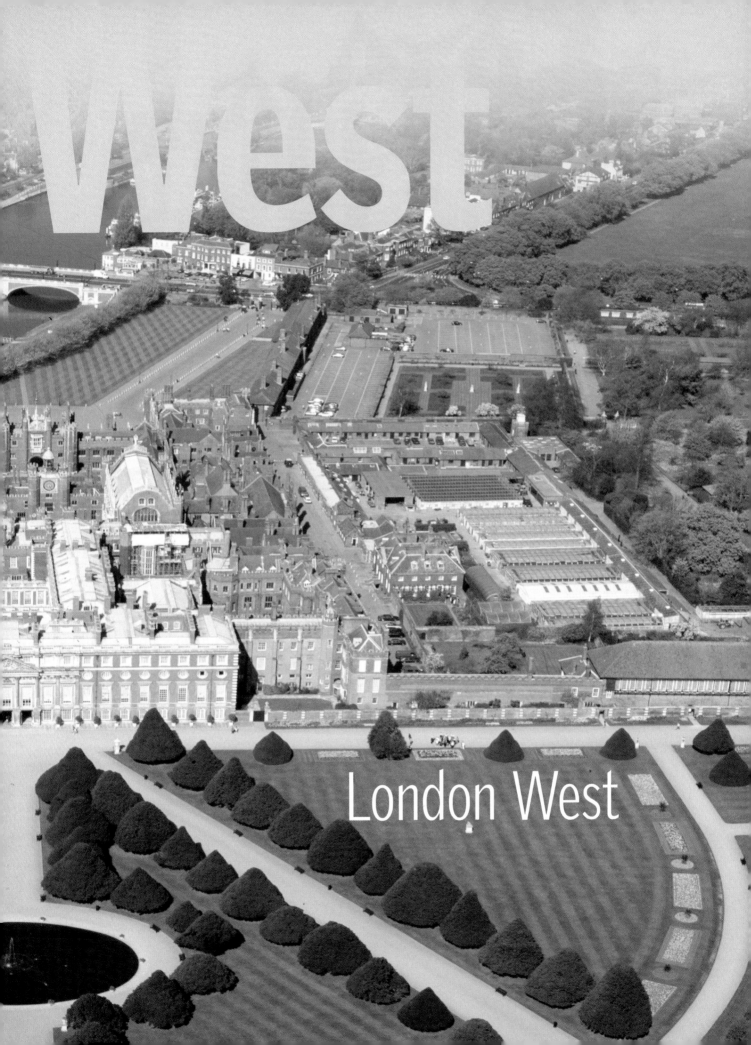

West

London West

Boston manor

 Jacobean house with fine
strapwork ceiling

Boston Manor Road, Brentford;
museum, open part year

Boston Manor survives. This in itself is
remarkable, cowering as it does barely 400
yards from the elevated section of the M4.
Traffic thunders past exquisite ceilings and
radiant overmantels, protected only by thin walls
and a grove of cedars.

Boston came to the public in good order.
The Clitherow family, owners since 1670, sold it
and its park to the Borough of Brentford in
1923. The manor was a modest Jacobean
structure first built by Lady Reade in 1623. This
original house appears to have been refaced with
classical vigour probably by James Clitherow, a
City merchant, who bought it in 1670. The
building is of redbrick with bold classical
window surrounds and a heavy cornice line. This
makes Boston another Carolean mansion, like
Forty Hall (see page 93), displaying the influence
of Inigo Jones, with whose classical imports its
anonymous architect must have been familiar.

The entrance hall, behind an ugly Victorian
porch, is dominated by a neo-Jacobean screen to
the staircase, all bulbous pilasters and grotesques.
To the left is a dining room filled with pictures of
old Brentford. The library behind has a frame over
the fireplace in the style of Grinling Gibbons and
a fine early-Victorian border to its ceiling carrying
the Clitherow motto, 'Loyal yet Free'.

Boston's punch is upstairs in the state drawing
room. This is one of the most remarkable
chambers in London. Its ceiling dates from the
original house in 1623 and is a work of the most
delicate Jacobean strapwork, panels and roundels,
all in low relief. Its creator is believed to be
Edward Stanyon, author of a similar work at
Blickling Hall, in Norfolk. The roundels depict the
Senses and the Virtues, complemented by a huge
chimneypiece, rising through the cornice to the
ceiling. The overmantel, set in a swirling field of
blue, white and gold, depicts Abraham and Isaac.
The room is sadly devoid of furniture.

An equally enjoyable ceiling is next door in the
bedroom. Here the strapwork pays homage to
Hope in the central roundel. Over the fireplace is a
portrait of an 18th-century Clitherow by Kneller.
The stairs have original Jacobean balusters,
repeated in paint on the walls. On the upper
flights are remarkable 18th-century wallpapers
depicting classical ruins.

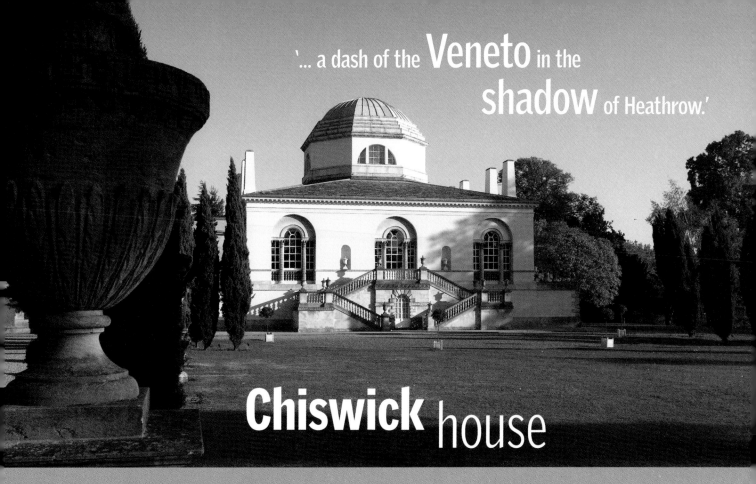

'... a dash of the Veneto in the shadow of Heathrow.'

Chiswick house

★★★★☆ Lord Burlington's Palladian pavilion

Burlington Lane, London W4; English Heritage, open all year

To most Londoners, Chiswick is a place of traffic jams on the way from the west and Heathrow Airport into London proper. It is a shame that Chiswick House cannot be part of the welcome. The house is the showpiece of the 18th-century Palladian revival, a dash of the Veneto in the valley of the shadow of Heathrow.

Like Inigo Jones's exemplary Queen's House at Greenwich of a century before, Chiswick was primarily for show. Begun c1725, it was a pavilion for old Chiswick House to its east, owned by the 3rd Earl of Burlington. The Earl had already established himself as the doyen of Grand Tour taste for the incoming Hanoverian Court, eager to restore the principles of Palladian design imported by Jones, and to rebut what he saw as the degenerate Baroque of Wren and Vanbrugh.

Burlington was a rigorous antiquarian and copious collector of books and drawings. He saw himself not as a radical innovator but a purist, returning architecture to the classical principles from which the school of Wren had departed. It was a battle in which Burlington was fiercely opposed, and ridiculed, by William Hogarth, who depicted him as a Continental fop undermining the roast beef of Old England. But Burlington was new, rich and Whig. Hogarth was Tory and poor. Burlington won and Hogarth lost.

Much debate has surrounded Burlington's sources for Chiswick. They include two Palladio villas in the Veneto, a masonic temple, Inigo Jones's drawings and the works of Vitruvius, Serlio and other Renaissance authors. The entrance is graced with a portico, dome and obelisks to conceal the chimney flues. The proportions are balanced, the elevations discreet and the walls a dazzling white stucco. External embellishment is confined to a beautiful grouping of steps up to the first floor.

Access is from the basement level, its service rooms now used for museum display. Upstairs is the heart of the composition, a domed octagonal saloon, with a ceiling whose panels diminish in size

Left The Blue Velvet Room was used by Lord Burlington as his study. It was one of three rooms at Chiswick created by William Kent that were hung with coloured velvets. **Above** The saloon is beneath the dome at the heart of the house. Kent lined the dome with panels similar to those he used in the Cupola Room at Kensington Palace.

back to London as his protégé. Burlington succeeded in getting Kent, nicknamed 'il Signior', to supplant Hogarth's father-in-law, Sir James Thornhill, at Kensington Palace (see page 56). This further fuelled Hogarth's hatred.

Each of Kent's rooms at Chiswick displays his eclectic virtuosity. The Red, Blue and Green Velvet Rooms have had their original wall coverings restored, albeit in wallpaper. The ceiling of the Red Velvet Room depicts the Triumph of the Arts. The Blue Velvet Room, based on a study in the Duke of Mantua's palace, is crowned with huge console brackets and an allegorical depiction of Architecture.

At the far end of the interior is the gallery, intended not just as a museum of Italian architecture but also as an exposition of its genesis. Here the eternal verities of European civilization were to be explained, with their attendant gods and muses in harmony with Nature. Northern heaviness was rejected in favour of Mediterranean refinement, that of the well-travelled Renaissance gentleman. The order is Corinthian, most developed of the classical orders and here attributed to the baskets of foliage carried on the heads of the gods.

Chiswick later passed to the Cavendish family, who demolished the old house next door and added two wings to the pavilion in the 1780s to extend the new house. When Walter Scott visited it in 1828 he found a garden party 'resembling a picture by Watteau' taking place. It was attended by a giant elephant. Chiswick House began a long decline, eventually serving as a lunatic asylum. It passed to the local council in 1928, and then to English Heritage. It has been meticulously restored and filled with many of Burlington's original pictures, including works by Ricci, Mytens and Guido Reni.

The gardens created by William Kent and Burlington were on the formal lines of classical landscape, based on a *patte d'oie* or goose foot of avenues radiating from a *rond point*. Each avenue had an architectural feature at its end. Nature was here fashioned into straight lines, a tradition with which Capability Brown was to break dramatically later in the century.

towards the centre, giving an illusion of height. The walls are decorated with classical busts and Old Master paintings. To Palladio such a room was for 'feast, entertainments, decorations, comedies, weddings and such like recreations'.

Round this saloon are chambers square, rectangular and octagonal. They are decorated by William Kent, the Yorkshire-born artist, architectural draughtsman and designer whom Burlington met in Italy in 1715 and brought

Chiswick: Hogarth's house

⭐ Redbrick Georgian house and country retreat of the popular 18th-century artist

Hogarth Lane, London W4; museum, open part year

Hogarth so detested Lord Burlington that it seems perverse of him in 1749 to buy a house next to Burlington's pavilion at Chiswick. Burlington was everything Hogarth was not, rich, stylish, influential and a commander of cultural fashion. Hogarth's print, *The Man of Taste*, depicted Burlington as foreign and immoral. Hogarth had no time for Whig dandies with Italian habits. In her biography of Hogarth, Jenny Uglow suggests the move to Chiswick was 'as if he were both laying claim to the territory, like an invader, and making peace after Kent's death the year before'. William Kent had been his real *bête noire*.

Fashion sided with Burlington, and so has history. While Chiswick House (see page 113) drips with English Heritage gold, Hogarth's House is neglected. The old lane has been wiped out by the Great West Road. The approach to the M4 passes roughly six feet from Hogarth's bedroom. An old mulberry tree, blasted by a wartime bomb, clings desperately to life. I expect one day to drive past and see the old place sighing and collapsing to the ground.

The redbrick building was little more than two rooms upstairs and two down. Hogarth installed a Venetian oriel window, the only feature to survive dereliction in the 19th century. Not until 1904 was the house rescued by the local council and reopened as a museum. The interiors have been restored with Georgian panelling but little else. No attempt is made to re-create the house as Hogarth would have known it.

The rooms are galleries of Hogarth prints, interspersed with illustrated boards about his life and work, excellently done if overly didactic. The final print is Bathos – Old Man Time, dying at the World's end with wreckage all round him. Hogarth might have offered it as comment on the turmoil outside.

Fenton house

★★★ Late 17th-century splendour, high on the hills above London

Windmill Hill, London NW3; National Trust, open part year

The enclave round Fenton House is a Hampstead haven. Modern flats retreat, ancient walls and trees step forward and grass verges keep cars at bay. To the east of Fenton House, there is a tiny path through the trees, hiding a dogs' graveyard. We might be in deep countryside.

The house was built by 1693, the date on a chimneystack, and is a compact William-and-Mary residence surprisingly little altered over the years. Its name derives from Philip Fenton, a Baltic merchant, who bought it in 1793. His son, James, was an early champion of 'not in my backyard', convening a meeting in the Hollybush Tavern in 1829 to fight successfully against any further development of adjacent Hampstead Heath.

'We might be **in deep countryside.'**

to face the road after 1800 and given a cheerful colonnade.

The interior remains as in the Fenton era, a friendly pile of twisted balusters, crowded alcoves and warm panelling, all redecorated in the 1970s by John Fowler. Each vista seems blessed with a harpsichord, spinet or virginals, often with a student practising. Similar sounds should be compulsory in all such properties, for a Georgian house would seldom have lacked for music. Fenton House is a place of bustles and bonnets, tripping feet and twittering voices, pride and prejudice.

The main dining room is now used for concerts, and contains the biggest harpsichord built in England, a Burckhardt Shudi of 1770. Other rooms are devoted to the porcelain collection. On the first floor is a rare gem, a London drawing room still with its 18th-century appearance. It has satinwood furniture, embroidered firescreens, needlework and Worcester. The former Blue Porcelain Room is now furnished as Lady Binning's bedroom, excellently displaying yet more of her needlework and porcelain.

Even better, Fenton House has its attics open to the public, from which there are marvellous views over London. Few visitors penetrate these rooms. To look out from them with the sound of music filtering up from below is to enjoy a moment's private communion with the city beneath. More could be made of the garden, especially given its inheritance of terrace walk and sunken rose garden.

The house was bequeathed to the National Trust in 1952 by the then owner, Lady Binning. The gift came with her furniture and collection of porcelain, and was merged with the Benton Fletcher collection of musical instruments. These were given to the Trust in 1937 by an army major who held that music should always be played on contemporary instruments. The porcelain and the instruments charmingly co-exist to form the house's personality.

The roofs are steep-pitched with a balcony, a design so common in the neighbourhood as to merit the term 'Hampstead balcony'. The old entrance faced south, as is clear from the approach through superb gates by Jean Tijou. The façade here is of seven bays but with odd narrow windows in the outer bays, a 17th-century device to light the smaller closets beyond the bedrooms. The entrance was moved

Freud's house

20 Maresfield Gardens, London, NW3; museum, open all year

When Sigmund Freud escaped Nazi Vienna for London in 1938 it led the news. He was Austria's most famous expatriate and he rightly chose Hampstead. 'Freud flees to Knightsbridge' would have been incongruous. He was by now an old man and his family, already in Britain, sought a bright, happy house in which he might continue his work. Maresfield Gardens was sunny, 'far too beautiful for us,' he said. He brought with him much of his furniture and books, as well as his treasured collection of antiquities. Sadly he had just one year to live.

Freud's family left the house untouched, a decision diluted by their also making it into a centre of Freud studies. The guidebook calls it 'a cult site, a place of mythic memory ... which continues to pulse to a lively current of problems and challenges'. This has laid the heavy hand of education on the place. Two upstairs rooms are used for videos, art exhibitions and lectures.

The house is an inter-war redbrick building in a most un-Viennese Queen Anne style. Only two rooms evoke the master's presence, the study/library on the ground floor and his daughter Anna's room on the first floor.

The study is as he left it, lined with books and display cases, heavy with Biedermeier furniture and the trappings of a 19th-century intellectual. Spectacles remain on the desk. That favourite Proustian relic of shrine custodians, an unfinished cigar, remains in an ashtray. The couch, claimed as 'the most famous piece of furniture in the world', awaits another patient, covered with cushions and carpets. At one end of it stands the almost as famous chair. Everywhere are statues, masks, busts and cases of figurines.

Freud's eagerness to collect significant objects caused him much concern. 'The core of paranoia,' he wrote, 'is the detachment of the libido from objects. A reverse course is taken by the collector who directs his surplus libido on to an inanimate object: a love of things.' Things were less fickle in their love than people. Freud compared his objects with a placid dog.

The work of Freud's daughter, Anna, on child analysis spread into other houses in the neighbourhood, but she kept Maresfield Gardens as a memorial to her father, transferring it to a charity before her death in 1982. Her room upstairs has her desk and bookshelves, as well as her beloved weaving loom. The room also contains painted chests and cupboards, as if from the Austrian countryside. The mix of Biedermeier and simple Austrian vernacular is one of the charms of the house.

On shelves everywhere are notices relating dreams familiar to Freud scholars, complete with context and interpretation. Hence we are given the sibling rivalry dream, the cupboard dream, the wild beast dream and the weaving dream. They are strangely discomforting. I take that to be the point.

Below Freud's famous couch was brought to London from the family's Vienna home. It was reputed to have been given to Freud by a grateful patient, Madame Benvenisti, in around 1890. Patients would recline on the couch, their heads propped up by pillows, while Freud sat out of sight behind them in his green tub chair.

Fulham palace

★★ Remains of the medieval episcopal palace of the Bishops of London

Bishop's Avenue, London SW6; museum, open all year

Palace by name but municipal events facility by nature, Fulham Palace is a London shocker. The former country seat of the Bishops of London, easily accessible by water to Lambeth and Westminster, saw its first building in the 12th century. It remains one of the capital's most important surviving medieval groupings. At the time of writing, a restoration project is in progress.

The bishop's estate was once big. Its moat was a mile long, the longest in England, enclosing 36 acres of ornamental and kitchen gardens. This moat was filled in with rubble in the 1920s and should be reinstated. The bishop did not move out until 1973, although by then he occupied only a flat in what was a fast decaying establishment. The estate still runs from the old church near Putney Bridge to the Fulham Football Ground at Craven Cottage. A lease was granted to Hammersmith and Fulham Council.

The palace is two linked buildings, one early Tudor, the other mid-Georgian, arranged round two courtyards. The most interesting is the Tudor one, essentially that of a 15th-century house with gatehouse, courtyard, porch and Great Hall. There is a delightful fountain in the middle. Each of the ranges defies dating, the guidebook listing six different building periods for the entrance range alone.

The Great Hall is originally of 1480, but became a Georgian drawing room and a chapel, before reverting to serve as a hall in the 19th century. Its classical screen with open pediment comes from a demolished building in the City. Beyond are corridors and the

Above The ornate Rococo ceiling of Bishop Sherlock's dining room at Fulham Palace dates from c1750. Now fully restored, the delicate plasterwork lay hidden for more than 40 years behind a false ceiling. At the centre of the pediment above the door is the coat of arms of the Bishops of London.

suite of large reception rooms added in the 18th century. Some have Rococo plasterwork ceilings but little else beyond a view over the gardens. This Georgian wing (which includes a small local museum) is best viewed from the garden and is open to the public. The Gothick north façade retains pretty traceried windows, recalling the rebuilding of this part of the palace by Stiff Leadbetter in 1764. The elevations were given a further, classical, dressing by S. P. Cockerell in 1814, sedate and dull.

The formal grounds were among the most extensive and exotic in London but were mostly destroyed in the landscaping of the 1760s. The Tudor walled garden survives, with a superb wisteria, as do fine trees planted by generations of bishops. The ghosts of episcopal grandeur still haunt this remarkable place. The council owners of Fulham have ambitious plans for the palace. They are urgently needed.

Grim's *dyke*

★ ★ Artist's house by Norman Shaw, later home to the famous librettist, W. S. Gilbert

Old Redding, Harrow; now a hotel

Frederick Goodall, the landscape painter, bought this spectacular site high on the Harrow Weald from the pickle magnate, Charles Blackwell, in 1856. He waited fourteen years before starting work on a romantic neo-Tudor house amid woods of pine and birch. Goodall's architect was Richard Norman Shaw, who insisted on changing the name to 'Graeme's Dyke', averse to the word 'grim' being attached to his cheerful style of architecture. He would have been appalled to learn that it was later chosen as a film venue for Vincent Price's 'The Cry of the Banshee' and Boris Karloff's 'The Curse of the Crimson Altar'.

In 1880 Goodall sold the house, which was bought in 1890 by W. S. Gilbert (of Gilbert and Sullivan). Gilbert changed the name back to Grim and commissioned the firm of Ernest George & Peto to make alterations. Gilbert came to love the place, filling it with friends and a menagerie of animals. He died after a swimming accident in the lake in 1911. The house is now a hotel, vigorously committed to keeping Gilbert's memory alive.

To Shaw's biographer, Andrew Saint, Grim's Dyke is a perfect example of a suave and approachable country house, 'like some Victorian fruit cake, full of rich and diverse ingredients ... perfect for the afternoon of British bourgeois civilization'. Sweeping roofs crown rich half-timbered

neo-Jacobean timbering, with split-level landings for Shaw's favourite conceit, the 'staircase greeting'.

The chief chamber of Goodall's house was his studio, in the form of a medieval 'Great Hall' elevated to the mezzanine level and turned on the house's axis for north–south light. Shaw designed it with a wagon roof and minstrels' gallery. Gilbert converted it to a grand reception room with a massive neo-Flemish alabaster fireplace. Photographs of the room at the time show it cluttered

walls. Mullioned windows soar through two storeys and rolling lawns stretch to meet enveloping woods. The style was to be repeated on a lesser scale in a thousand north-west London semis, and across the burgeoning suburbs of the English-speaking world.

The house interiors are surprisingly domestic. The entrance lobby is that of a suburban villa. Off the hall is a dining room with inglenook, and a drawing room and library with spacious windows overlooking the lawn. The stairs are a feature in themselves, a mass of

with heavy curtains, chandeliers and a forest of drooping palms. Today the room is a restaurant, the walls lined with pictures of Gilbert-and-Sullivan productions, some of hilarious campness. Off to one side is Gilbert's rehearsal room, what he called his 'flirtarium'.

Grim's Dyke was a favourite haunt of Sir John Betjeman, the Bard of Metroland, as this part of London was once known. I once caught him here, besieged by a lunch party of elderly ladies, beaming with pleasure under the roof of one of his favourite architects.

Gunnersbury park

★ Rothschild mansion set in landscaped grounds

Pope's Lane, London W3; museum, open all year

If Fulham Palace is sad, Gunnersbury is sadder. The former Rothschild mansion, sandwiched between the North Circular and the M4 at Brentford, should be as dignified and well appointed as that family's other seats in Buckinghamshire. At the very least, it should be a decent hotel.

Today, the park is well tended but the house is a poverty-stricken museum and education centre. Terraces along which Victorian guests once glided past Georgian temples and looked out towards the hills of Surrey weep with neglect. The windows are now blind with shutters. The grand rooms are boxed in with display cases.

The original 17th-century house was built by John Webb for a prominent Stuart lawyer, Sir John Maynard, and later taken by Princess Amelia, daughter of George II. The grounds were laid out in the 18th century but the main house was demolished in 1801 and two adjacent mansions built in its place. The larger house, Gunnersbury Park, was bought by Nathan Rothschild in 1835 and passed to his son, Lionel, Britain's first Jewish MP. The architect, Sydney Smirke, added a series of reception rooms along the south side of the house overlooking the park. The second house, known as Gunnersbury House, was bought in 1889 for the use of guests. The two houses reached their apotheosis in the late-Victorian period, but even the Rothschilds had too many properties and sold the entire estate to the local council in 1925, in whose hands it remains.

The exterior of the house remains impressive, at least viewed from the south (above), with a two-storeyed stucco façade and a central colonnade. Inside, Smirke's three reception rooms survive, adorned with scagliola columns and heavy classical ceilings. The central drawing room has a painted ceiling panel of The Four Seasons by Edmond Parris, recently restored. A collection of Rothschild carriages incongruously fills the drawing room.

Left Leather fire buckets, possibly dating from the 17th century, hang at ceiling height along the west passage leading to Ham's Great Hall. Stairs from this corridor descend to the basement kitchen, hence the fire buckets here would have been a sensible precaution.

Elizabeth Murray was larger than life. She was daughter of William Murray, Earl of Dysart and whipping boy to Charles I. A contemporary account describes her as 'of great beauty but of far greater parts, a wonderful quickness of apprehension and an amazing vivacity in conversation'. But there was a sting in the tail, 'what ruined these accomplishments, she was restless in her ambition, profuse in her expense and of a most ravenous covetousness'.

Elizabeth married a Tollemache and, on his death, married the Earl of Lauderdale, reputedly saving his life during the Civil War by flirting with Cromwell. She dominated both her husbands. Lauderdale rose to a dukedom, shining briefly as the L of the Restoration Cabal. To Bishop Burnet, he had a 'tongue too big for his mouth and his

Ham house

★★★★ Jacobean mansion with Restoration improvements

Ham Street, Richmond; National Trust, open part year, gardens open all year

whole manner rough and boisterous, and very unfit for Court'. He died in disgrace in 1682. Lely's portrait of the couple in the house cannot avoid showing him arrogant and ugly and her wilful and calculating.

Ham was the house, first built in 1610, which Elizabeth inherited from her father and which she and Lauderdale struggled to convert into a place worthy of a courtier. Altered and extended by William Samwell in 1672, it was to be one of the first houses with a 'modern' promenade of so-called state rooms on the first floor. There was a matching family set on the ground floor. After Elizabeth's death, her Tollemache descendants did not alter or embellish her work. What we see is mostly still hers.

Today, no London house so embodies the transience of greatness. Mighty oaks and attendant crows still guard the shades of the departed Duchess on her foggy Thames bank. The building sits well back from the river within its gardens and grounds. No suburban estate presses close. The earlier house had been an E-plan, with a tower over the porch and projecting turrets. The Lauderdales removed the tower and turrets and adorned the entrance façade with a row of classical busts in niches. They decided not to alter the off-centre location of the hall, but added their new state rooms overlooking the garden to the rear.

The contrast between the intimacy of the ground floor and the grandeur of the first is the charm of Ham. Downstairs, one might be tiptoeing through a de Hooch painting, the atmosphere strongly Dutch. Sun streams past warm oak onto black-and-white tiles. On the

'... no London house **so embodies** the transience of **greatness.**'

walls of the Duchess's rooms are seascapes by the younger van de Velde. The Duke's Room is hung with black and gold damask. In the White Closet is a Danckerts of them both receiving guests in the ostentatious presence of classical statues. Everywhere is Dutch pottery, Dutch tulip vases and wood from the Dutch East Indies.

The first floor is reached by Murray's old staircase, its balustrade panels of 1637 still portraying not classical scenes but battle trophies. Beneath is a small family chapel. At the top of the stairs a picture gallery overlooks the hall below. Here hangs the Lely of the Lauderdales and, for contrast, one of Elizabeth as a demure young lady.

The North Drawing Room dates from Murray's house, big-boned and Carolean. It has a heavy coffered ceiling and a Bernini-esque fireplace surround with massive twisted pilasters. The room is hung with Mortlake tapestries. Beyond is a dark, green closet, fashioned into a Cabinet of Miniatures or small museum.

Below Earlier silk wall hangings in the North Drawing Room were replaced in 1904 by a set of Mortlake tapestries dating from the early 18th century that depict the months of the year. The chairs were probably bought by the Duchess of Lauderdale in Paris in the 1670s; they are known as the Dolphin suite after the carvings on the arms.

Above The book-lined library contains two globes dating from c1746 – one celestial, the other terrestrial – plus two mahogany pole screens, each covered with a glazed map.
Below The 'sleeping chair' in the Queen's Closet could be lowered to allow the sitter to recline.

The Long Gallery also survives from Murray's house. It is splendidly dark, filled with 22 Stuart portraits flanked by giant pilasters. Beyond is Lauderdale's library of 1674, said to be the earliest private house library extant in England, once including books by Caxton. It is a most scholarly room. The man cannot have been all vulgarity.

Along the south front of the house run the Lauderdales' state rooms. The sequence is of ante-chamber, Queen's Bedchamber and the beautiful Queen's Closet. The last is the jewel of Ham, with a Verrio ceiling and scagliola fireplace surround. An arch thick with acanthus frames a dais and 'sleeping chair'. The rooms were prepared for a visit from Charles II's queen, Catherine, which is believed never to have happened.

The National Trust has been good to Ham, although it needs a family in residence. Can some modern Tollemaches not be summoned to reoccupy the upper floors? As Queen Charlotte wrote on a visit in 1809, the place is 'beautiful and magnificent both within and without, but truly melancholy'.

'Hampton Court has something for **every taste.**'

Hampton Court is a palace of two eras. At the front (this page) it is decidedly Tudor; to the rear (opposite page) it is quintessentially a William-and-Mary building.

Hampton Court palace

★★★★☆ Wolsey's great palace, taken over by Henry VIII and converted by William and Mary

Hampton Court Way, East Molesey; museum, open all year

If Windsor is the grandest of England's royal houses, Hampton Court is the most seductive. Its Tudor profile, its forest of chimneys, its mix of intimate chambers and grand state rooms answer to every emotion. Whether shimmering above the river in summer or set about with winter snow, its entrance is the epitome of the flamboyant and tyrannical Henry VIII. To the rear is a jolly William-and-Mary building crammed with chambers in the Dutch style. Hampton Court has something for every taste.

The great palace, built on the site of a manor owned by the Hospitallers of St John, was begun in 1515 when the forty-year-old Wolsey was already Lord Chancellor. The centre of his house was set round Clock Court. Hampton Court was one of the largest houses in northern Europe in its day, based on a layout approved for cardinals. It is still one of England's most complete Tudor 'townships', more extensive even than Knole, in Kent. The courts alone include Master Carpenter's Court, Lord Chamberlain's Court, Fish Court, Chapel Court and Round Kitchen Court. The palace could house a retinue of 500. Shortly before his demise, Wolsey entertained '14 score beds provided and furnished'.

Hampton Court was handed over to Henry VIII in 1528 by Wolsey after his fall from grace for failing to secure Henry's divorce from Catherine of Aragon. Henry continued to extend and embellish it, but after his death the palace was neglected for over a century until it caught the imagination of William III and Queen Mary, who had Wren plan its rebuilding. They ran out of time and money but the palace was occupied by Queen Anne and partly rebuilt by George II. No monarch has lived at Hampton since. Although it was accessible via a (well-tipped) house-keeper, the palace was opened free of charge by Queen Victoria in 1838. By 1850, 200,000 people a year were going to see it.

Henry left Wolsey's famous entrance façade and gatehouse, with Giovanni da Maiano's medallions of Roman emperors, but rebuilt the Great Hall and the chapel, to the left of the inner Clock Court. The hall is still the largest room in the palace, its massive hammerbeam roof crowded with carvings and pendants. The tapestries, regarded as the finest of the 16th century in England, were woven in Brussels of gold and silver thread.

Adjacent to the hall is the Great Watching Chamber, where retainers slept and ate. The Haunted Gallery beyond is said to echo with the screams of Catherine Howard, searching vainly for her husband to protest her innocence of adultery. Her execution was Henry's ugliest act, unredeemed by the Holbein portrait of him that hangs in the gallery.

The Chapel Royal is a spectacular room, with Henry's Tudor ceiling rich in ribs and pendants, looking down on Wren's reredos carved by Grinling Gibbons. Next to the chapel is the Chapel Court, site of Henry's tennis court. These are the oldest parts of the palace, worth seeking out away from the tourist crush. They include secret courts and yards, breweries, cellars and kitchens, crammed with ancient cooking utensils.

From here we burrow deeper into the palace and find the other Hampton Court, that of Wren and his successors. Fountain Court is a Baroque work reflecting William's desire to create a memory of his palace of Het Loo in Holland. Wren was so criticized for the court's smallness that William had to take the blame himself. The court is surrounded by not one set of state rooms but two, an expense necessitated by William and Mary being joint monarchs and thus requiring separate and equal 'precedence'. Their palace, therefore, has not one but two royal staircases, two guard

chambers, presence chambers, bedchambers, withdrawing chambers and closets.

The King's apartments are the grander, approached under Wren's screen in Clock Court, classical pomp inserted beneath a flurry of Tudor chimneys. The staircase is pure monarchical glorification, England's answer to Bernini's Scala Regia at the Vatican. It is entirely covered in murals by Antonio Verrio, depicting William as Alexander the Great, worshipped by the gods of Plenty. (This for a man who owed his throne to rejecting James II's divine right of kings!)

The landing commences the enfilade of the King's state rooms, three throne rooms followed by two bedrooms, all hung with massive tapestries. The state bed is so big that the King apparently used the smaller one next door in which to sleep. In this he was assisted by exquisite works of Chinese and Japanese porcelain and a Verrio ceiling of Mars in the lap of Venus. The rooms were restored facsimile after a fire in 1986, defying misguided pleas from the Royal Institute of British Architects to rebuild 'in the style of our time'.

A flight of stairs leads down to the ground floor and a series of furnished closets beneath. The contrast with upstairs is total. This is where the King lived day to day. These might be the rooms of any late 17th-century country house, except that each has a surprise, a Gibbons overmantel, a van Dyck or lavish gold tableware.

The Queen's state apartments are marginally less grand than the King's, as completed by Queen Anne and then George II. Her staircase was painted by William Kent, the state rooms designed by Vanbrugh. The first of these, the Guard Chamber, has an extraordinary fireplace by Gibbons, the overmantel supported by two giant Yeomen of the Guard. The Queen's state bedchamber has its original Georgian bed. Like the King, the Queen also enjoyed a suite of non-state rooms, here overlooking Fountain Court. They were built for her by Wren but not

'The hall is still the **largest**
room in the **palace** ...'

Left The staircase that leads to King William's Apartments rises up through a series of wall paintings by Antonio Verrio. The composition is based on one of the *Satires* by the 4th-century writer Julian the Apostate, and represents the triumph of Alexander the Great; it serves as an allegory for William's triumph over the Stuarts.
Right Verrio also painted the ceiling of the King's Great Bedchamber. It shows Endymion asleep in the arms of Morpheus, the Greek god of dreams. The room's purpose was mainly ceremonial; William was dressed here each morning in the company of a few privileged courtiers.

fitted out until 1716, for the future George II and his wife, Caroline. They are the most intimate and enjoyable chambers in the palace. Her bedroom appears to be the only one in the place where King and queen could sleep together in private (producing ten children). Here the Queen performed her toilet, took tea with friends and prayed in her private oratory.

To reach these rooms, the visitor must pass along the so-called Communication Gallery – built to enable William and Mary eventually to reach each other – and the Cartoon Gallery. The one is now hung with Lelys of court beauties, the other with copies of the Raphael cartoons now at the V&A. This range of so-called Georgian Rooms ends in the Cumberland Suite, which was converted by William Kent for George II's son, the Duke of Cumberland, on his reaching the diminutive age of ten. His bedroom has a columned alcove for a small bed, flanked by doors leading to closets.

Behind these quarters, we can also see another fragment of Wolsey's palace, the tiny Wolsey Closet with an exquisite Tudor ceiling and murals of the Passion of Christ. It is a gem of the early English Renaissance.

Hampton Court is truly vast. Back in the Clock Court is the entrance to more of Wolsey's palace, the rooms hung with Renaissance paintings. Outside in the Orangery is Mantegna's epic, *The Triumphs of Caesar*, bought from the Gonzagas by Charles I and kept at Hampton Court ever since. William's Banqueting House in the Privy Garden is painted throughout by Verrio. The Great Vine still grows in the greenhouse and the parterres are restored.

After visiting the house, there is nothing more restful than to walk by the river and to lose oneself in the great park to the east.

Keats house

'Few London houses so well encapsulate

★★ Romantic poet's last home in England

Keats Grove, London NW3; museum, open all year

Does a happier house tell a sadder tale? In 1818, the twenty-three-year-old John Keats came to live in half the home that his friend, Charles Brown, had built on the southern slopes of Hampstead. Here he could commune with nature and visit Leigh Hunt and his friends in the Vale of Health. 'To one who has been long in city pent,' he wrote, ''Tis very sweet to look into the fair/ And open face of heaven.'

During his tenure of what was called Wentworth House, the other half of the 'semi' was rented by a young widow, Mrs Brawne, and her three children. Keats was soon infatuated with one of them, Fanny Brawne, and the couple became engaged in the autumn of 1819. It was a brief romance. Next year, Keats was ill with consumption and, despite the Brawnes' nursing, left for Rome and death in 1821. In her essay on the house, Margaret Drabble gives it 'a tragic lightness, a playful brittle terror'.

The small Regency building is still as Keats would have known it, although the garden is now surrounded by development. How Keats and Brown contrived to live cheek by jowl with the Brawnes,

JOHN KEATS
1795–1821

Orphaned at the age of 15, Keats was obliged to pursue a career in medicine, but he was always drawn to literature and in 1814 began writing poetry. In 1816, probably influenced by the editor Leigh Hunt who had published some of his early work, he gave up medicine in favour of poetry; his first book appeared in 1817.

At the end of 1818, Keats was caring for his consumptive brother, Tom. When Tom died, Keats moved to Hampstead. The year that followed is often referred to as his 'Great Year'. Inspired by sadness at his brother's death and by his love for Fanny, he wrote some of his greatest works – 'To Autumn', 'Ode to Psyche', 'Ode on Melancholy' and 'Ode to a Nightingale'.

By 1820, Keats himself was seriously ill with tuberculosis. He left for Italy to spend the winter in its milder climate, accompanied by his good friend Joseph Severn, who painted this portrait of Keats listening to a nightingale. The pair travelled to Rome and it was there, in a rented house on the Spanish Steps, that Keats died on 23 February 1821.

the contrast of city enclosure and open space.'

yet apart from them, is hard to envisage, especially before a Victorian extension was added to the east. Each household had just four rooms, two living rooms downstairs and two bedrooms upstairs. Keats's rooms are furnished more or less as he left them.

Upstairs is the tiny bedroom with the tented bed on whose pillow Keats noted the spots of coughed blood that, as a former medical student, he knew to be his 'death warrant'. In his sitting room downstairs he spent his final days in Hampstead, writing to Fanny next door and watching her walk in the garden. Outside is the tree under which, in 1819, he is said to have composed the 'Ode to a Nightingale'.

Few London houses so well encapsulate the contrast of city enclosure and open space. By the time Thomas Hardy visited the house, 'Streets have stolen up all around,/ And never a nightingale pours one/ Full-throated sound.' Today the place is a shrine. In one room is a small collection of memorabilia, including a copy of the sentimental picture (in the National Portrait Gallery) of Keats by Joseph Severn. The nightingale is in the background, silhouetted against the moon. Here too is a lock of Keats's hair. The house was rescued from demolition by American subscriptions and is now well guarded by the City Corporation.

Kenwood house

★★★ An Adam mansion with a famous art collection

Hampstead Lane, London NW3; English Heritage, open all year

Kenwood spreads itself generously across the heights of Hampstead Heath, as if to separate the quarrelling sisters of Hampstead and Highgate. I have known the house all my life and still find thrilling its sudden appearance on its hill from the woods beneath. This is London's most smiling mansion.

Kenwood was owned by a succession of Scottish noblemen until acquired by the Lord Chief Justice, the 1st Earl of Mansfield, in 1754, and remodelled ten years later by Robert Adam. He added a portico to the entrance and an exquisite library. Two later wings enclosed the entrance courtyard. Most of the furniture was sold in 1922 and the house was saved from demolition only by the Guinness magnate, Lord Iveagh, who bought it in 1925 and left it to the nation with his magnificent art collection in 1927. The park was incorporated into Hampstead

Right One of the great treasures of Lord Iveagh's legacy is Vermeer's *Guitar Player*, which hangs in the dining room at Kenwood. On 23 February 1974, the painting was stolen by IRA sympathisers who threatened to burn it unless two hunger strikers in Brixton prison were moved to Northern Ireland to complete their sentences. The painting was found, unharmed, in a nearby churchyard ten weeks later.

'This is London's most
smiling mansion.'

Heath, a blessing beyond price. The house is now run by English Heritage, which is struggling to recover much that was sold in 1922.

Robert Adam, with Syon House and Osterley Park already built, had difficulties with Kenwood. To the south the sloping site forbad a proper portico and yielded a weak composition. The only enrichment is ten pilasters and a modest pediment, unbalanced by the wings but cheered by being coated in creamy stucco. The park is by Repton, with a lake and Adam bridge, leading to a diminutive modern concert stage.

The interior of Kenwood is gradually returning from art gallery to house. As yet, only the front hall and library vibrate with Adam exuberance. The latter is one of his richest interiors. The bays are filled with mirrors. Apses at each end are divided by screens of columns. 'Nothing can be more noble and striking when properly applied than a fine order of columns,' wrote Adam, yet nothing was 'more sterile and disgustful than to see for ever the dull repetition of Dorick, Ionick and Corinthian entablatures.' The ceilings are by Antonio Zucchi. It was at Kenwood, while painting the *Rape of Europa*, that tradition claims Zucchi fell in love with Angelica Kauffmann before carrying her off to Rome.

A lovely 1811 harp has been returned to the music room and a sideboard has been found in America and returned to the breakfast room. Adam's 'Chinese' chimneypiece in the Upper Hall is an astonishing work, architecturally plain but encrusted with mermen, gryphons and cherubs. In the rest of the house, screens, fireplaces and ceilings mainly inserted after Adam had departed must serve to decorate mostly empty rooms.

Besides that are the pictures. Kenwood contains one of the most enjoyable small collections in London, enhanced with the addition of the Suffolk collection of 16th-century court portraits from Ranger's House (see page 102). In the music room are English women, including Reynolds's *Mrs Masters as Hebe*, apparently intended 'to comfort her jealous husband'. Romney's Emma Hamilton is depicted as a saint. Gainsborough is represented by Lady Brisco, her hair about to take flight, and Mary, Countess Howe, an aristocrat in a whirlwind of pink satin and lace against a stormy background.

The dining room contains major Dutch works by van Dyck, Hals, Cuyp and a Rembrandt self-portrait. Here too is Vermeer's haunting *Guitar Player*, a caged bird apparently singing to a lover listening in the woods outside.

Kew palace

✩✩ Royal refuge of George III and his family

Kew Gardens, Kew; museum, open part year

This must be the most domestic 'palace' in London. Buried inside Kew Gardens, Kew Palace is a poignant place. It was here that the ailing George III retreated with his wife, Charlotte, as madness approached and before his removal to Windsor in 1805.

Queen Charlotte lived on in the house and two of the royal sons were married in the first-floor drawing room. The King and Queen had bought the house as an annexe to neighbouring Kew House (marked now by only a sundial) for use by their fifteen children. After the Queen's death in 1818, it was shut up for almost a century until being merged with Kew Gardens. A ten-year restoration project, begun in 1996, has transformed the house, returning many of the rooms to the style and comfort that the Royal Family would have enjoyed.

The house, on the bank of the Thames, was originally built by a merchant, Samuel Fortrey, in 1631. The style was emphatically Dutch, much favoured in the City of London in contrast to the Court preference for the southern Renaissance of Inigo Jones. Here the classicism is expressed in carved brick. The façade might be on a canal in Amsterdam, with double-curved gables and rusticated brick surrounds to the windows. After uncovering evidence that the house was once painted red, restorers have reinstated the bold exterior colour scheme.

'The façade might be on a **canal in Amsterdam ...**'

Above Princess Elizabeth's bedroom at Kew Palace has been re-created much as it would have been when she moved into the room in 1805; the reproduction carpet and Grecian couch-bed are based on contemporary designs. One wall in the room has been left unfinished, revealing the structure of the original house and a servant's doorway in one corner.

The interior is unpalatial. A cross-passage runs from front to back, with rooms on either side. To the left, an ante room leads into the King's Library, now arranged as a museum of royal private life at the palace. To the right lies the King's Dining Room, once part of the main hall in Fortrey's house. In refurnishing the room, restorers were guided by early 19th-century accounts that included bills of sale for cotton chintz curtains and a chamber organ. Next door is the King's Breakfast Room, which displays a tiny dolls' house, built in the 1780s for George III's daughters. In contrast to the bespoke grandeur of Queen Mary's dolls' house at Windsor (see page 31), this was furnished with fittings made or decorated by the young princesses themselves.

On the first floor are Queen Charlotte and Princess Elizabeth's rooms. Three of these have been decorated with a startling green verditer wallpaper with matching Greek-key border, faithfully re-created from fragments of the original 1805 decorative scheme uncovered behind a shutter.

The upper floors of the palace have been left untouched. Apartments occupied by two of the King's daughters are on display, the walls bare of decoration, the rooms unfurnished. The attic rooms and servants quarters are declared too fragile to be viewed by visitors.

Marble Hill house

★ ★ ★ Grand Georgian villa built for a royal favourite

Richmond Road, Twickenham; English Heritage, open all year

Henrietta Hobart was the orphaned daughter of Sir Henry Hobart of Blickling Hall, Norfolk. She was married in 1706 to Charles Howard, an improvident younger son of the Earl of Suffolk, then in the Dragoon Guards. The couple were always in debt and fled, like many adventurers, to Hanover to attach themselves to the court of the future George I.

With the Hanoverian succession in 1714, they returned to England in the royal retinue. Howard was attached to the King, Henrietta to the Prince and Princess of Wales. This involved her moving to Richmond following the Prince's estrangement from his father, George I, and 'exiled' up-river.

By 1720, the Prince was said to be going every evening to the thirty-two-year-old Mrs Howard's lodgings. Yet all gossip admitted that he regarded the lady 'rather as a necessary appurtenance to his grandeur as a Prince than an addition to his pleasures as a man'. There is no evidence of a physical relationship between them, indeed everyone, including the Prince's wife, seems to have approved of Henrietta. Walpole described her as being 'sensible, artful, agreeable but with neither sense nor art enough to make the king think her more agreeable than his wife'.

Separated from her husband and eager for a house of her own near Richmond, Henrietta persuaded George in 1724 to give her £11,500 for a building and furniture. He appointed trustees from his circle to select a site and supervise the design, including Lord Herbert and Lord Ilay. Also consulted were Colen Campbell and Roger Morris; Charles Bridgeman designed the gardens.

Right The chief reception room at Marble Hill House was known as the Great Room, where Henrietta Howard entertained in style. The paintings that decorate the room include several topographical works by the artist Giovanni Paulo Panini. He was renowned for his *vedute*, or 'view paintings', depicting real or imaginary views of Rome's classical ruins.

Seldom has so much talent been expended on so modest a property.

This may explain why the house took five years to build. Meanwhile, Henrietta's husband succeeded, by virtue of a lucky series of deaths of his brothers, to the Suffolk earldom and conveniently died. Henrietta, now a widowed countess, retired from Court, married George Berkeley and lived happily at Marble Hill until her death in 1767.

Today, Marble Hill peeps through the trees in the many views painted of the Thames upstream from Richmond Hill. It recalls the great days of Georgian Twickenham, with Augustan villas set in a rustic landscape with Walpole, Pope and the Hanoverian court gossips gliding by on barges. It is a handsome if plain box of white stucco.

The interior is planned round the Great Room, the reception room on the first floor. Visitors were intended to enter from an outside staircase in the manner of Chiswick House (see page 113), but this was never built. Instead they entered into the 'rustic', through a lower hall round which are arranged the dining and breakfast rooms.

The Great Room was where the Countess would have received her guests, in a style that suggested a much bigger mansion. Lord Herbert, as his contribution to the design, appears to have intended the room to have the proportions of Inigo Jones's Single Cube Room at his seat at Wilton House, Wiltshire. Its grand ceiling rises through the upper two storeys of the house.

The walls are lined with fine side tables, rediscovered in Australia in 1987. Robust gilded putti adorn the mantelpiece. Paintings of ancient Rome by Panini have also been restored to their frames over the doors. The Countess's bedroom has recently been rehung with green damask and refurnished, and the second floor gallery restored. Now, it all needs more pictures.

In 1901, the shipping tycoon, William Cunard, tried to demolish Marble Hill for housing. After a public outcry, he sold it instead to the London County Council, who merely neglected it. Restoration by English Heritage has restored its dignity, if not its vitality.

The grounds are used as local sports fields, but come to life with a concert programme each summer. The garden claims the tallest black walnut, bay willow and Italian alder in England.

Below and right All that now remains of the lost Thames-side mansion known as Orleans House, the Octagon is believed to have been built especially for a visit by Princess Caroline of Ansbach, wife of the future George II; the building is similar in style to pavilions then fashionable in palace gardens in her native Germany. The portrait busts around the dome and the medallions that decorate the walls inside include likenesses of George and Caroline.

Orleans house Octagon

⭐ Early Georgian garden pavilion by James Gibb

Riverside, Twickenham; museum, open all year

Orleans House was erected by the Thames in 1710 by James Johnston, Secretary of State for Scotland and immensely rich. Johnston's gardens were once reputed to yield 'the best collection of fruits of any gentleman in England'. In 1720 he added a pavilion by James Gibbs, reputedly to receive the then Princess of Wales. In 1815, the house was let to the exiled Duc d'Orléans, later King Louis Philippe, a distinction reflected in the house's name.

The shipping magnate, William Cunard, bought Orleans House and the adjacent Marble Hill in 1882, living in the former and later trying to demolish the latter for development. In 1926, his executors sold Orleans House to a gravel company for excavation. They pulled down the great house but found no gravel.

A local conservationist, Mrs Ionides, daughter of the founder of Shell, bought Gibbs's pavilion to save that too from destruction and to protect the sylvan view from Richmond Hill. She bequeathed it to the local council and it remains a delightful survivor in this sorely tried landscape.

The Octagon is a gem of early Georgian design, a single chamber with large windows on five sides and a fireplace and two doors on three. The doors are magnificent, worthy of the most sumptuous town house. Reclining figures and putti adorn the pediments. Medallions depict the then Prince and Princess of Wales. Graceful Corinthian pilasters mask the angles.

The ceiling is by Gibbs's stuccoists, Giuseppe Artari and Giovanni Bagutti, then working for him at St Martin-in-the-Fields. The dome carries exquisite Baroque decoration. It is a room of superb poise but in need of further restoration. To have contemplated destroying it is astonishing. Finding a new use for it is a challenge.

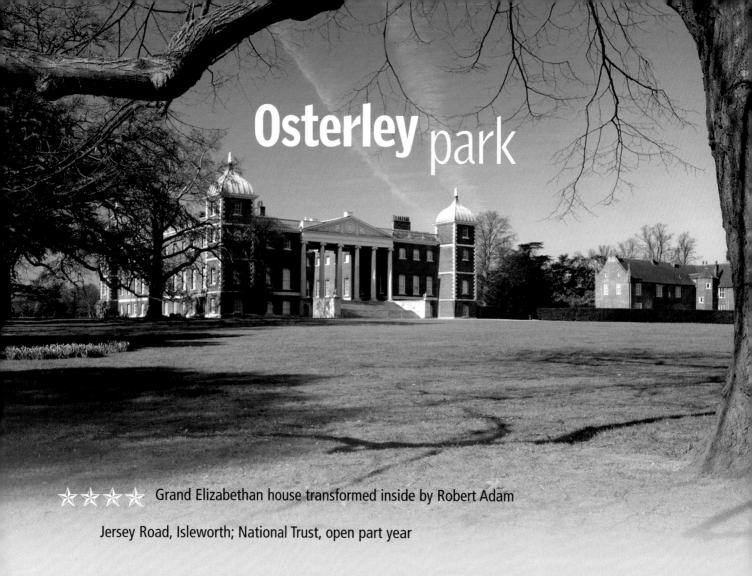

Osterley park

★★★★ Grand Elizabethan house transformed inside by Robert Adam

Jersey Road, Isleworth; National Trust, open part year

In 1576 Elizabeth I was being entertained at Osterley by its owner, London's premier merchant prince, Sir Thomas Gresham, founder of the Royal Exchange. She suggested in the course of the evening that his central courtyard would 'appear more handsome' with a wall across it. Between her going to bed and awakening next morning, Gresham's workmen built just that. Cynical contemporaries remarked that it was not the Queen, but 'money commandeth all things'.

The wall did not survive, nor did the house stay in the Gresham family for long. It passed to the London developer, Nicholas Barbon, and in 1713 to the banker, Francis Child. It was Child's descendants who remodelled the Elizabethan house, first using local craftsmen and then, in 1761, Robert Adam. The family insisted, like the Duke of Northumberland at Syon, that Adam merely remodel their old house and confine his talents to the interior. Adam's masterstroke was to enclose the courtyard with a pedimented loggia linking the north and south wings. The result enhances the serene symmetry of the redbrick exterior, which now floats like a ship on a sea of grass.

Of Adam's interior, Horace Walpole wrote from neighbouring Twickenham that it was 'so improved and enriched that all the Percies and Seymours of Sion must die of envy'. It is now a museum of Adam decoration, with some of the original furniture still in place. When Child's descendant, the 9th Earl of Jersey, gave the house to the National Trust in 1949 and fled into tax exile, he took the best pictures with him, works by Poussin, Rubens, Lorraine, van Dyck and Salvator Rosa. They were lost in a warehouse fire. Osterley's present paintings are on loan from the V&A.

Unlike its Adam cousins, Syon and Kenwood, the house remains at the centre of its original farming estate, with meadows and livestock as well as a lake and park. This fragment of rural

'The hall is a **glorious composition** of white and pale blue ...'

Middlesex survives, incredibly, sandwiched between the Great West Road and the M4. Jets rumble low overhead on the flight-path into nearby Heathrow. It is surreal.

Perhaps for that reason, Osterley is neglected. I have never seen it crowded and it is often empty. It is also one of the National Trust's most bloodless properties, victim of capture by earnest conservationists. Its blinds are drawn and rooms are in perpetual gloom. If something is not done to bring it to life, some future government will turn it into a First Class Terminal for Heathrow.

The plan is simple. A Roman entrance hall leads into a Long Gallery beyond, the main reception rooms running down each side. Completed over the course of the 1760s and 1770s, they display the evolution of Adam's style so vividly that his biographer, Eileen Harris, recommends that they be viewed in chronological rather than architectural order. The one-way traffic flow imposed by the Trust makes this impossible.

The hall is a glorious composition of white and pale blue, its walls crowded with giant trophies and its ceiling reflected in the floor beneath. Visitors are next ordered into a side wing to see the

Below When Adam created the hall at Osterley he had to work within a space with a relatively low ceiling, so he made use of architectural details to give an increased sense of height. Tall pilasters reach up nearly to the ceiling, supporting a narrow Greek-key frieze rather than the more usual deep entablature. Large stucco panels, depicting military trophies, intersperse the pilasters and further enhance their apparent length.

Above A tapestry of *Cupid and Psyche* hangs above the fireplace in the Tapestry Room; Psyche is dropping oil onto Cupid's wing to wake him. Other tapestries in the room depict the Loves of the Gods: *Venus and Vulcan, Aurora and Cephalus, Vertumnus and Pomona*. These three couples were intended to personify Fire, Air and Earth, respectively. The remaining element, Water, is represented by the pier-glass between the windows.

library. The bookcases here are boldly architectural, their leather bindings almost part of the decoration. The ceiling used to be painted in bright colours from pattern books found in the Soane Museum. Now it is white, current victor in the 'colour wars' fought by Adam experts. Over a mantelpiece is a picture by Antonio Zucchi of Catullus writing an *Epitaph on the Death of his Mistress's Bird*. I wonder how many bankers would commission that subject today.

The adjacent staircase had to be squeezed into a wing of the Tudor house, a constraint turned by Adam to brilliant effect. The stair rises to the landing past a tall Corinthian screen with honeysuckle balusters. The ceiling was filled with a canvas by Rubens, removed by Jersey and lost in the fire. The present version is a copy. The upstairs rooms include a fine Adam bed with taffeta hangings. In Mrs Child's dressing room is a Rococo chimneypiece displaying porcelain, its oval frame dipping into the mantelpiece below.

Adam was attentive to the social behaviour of the English house. He lavished attention on dining rooms and libraries, holding that the former should have neither panelling nor fabric, which would retain the smell of food. Libraries should have no carpets, since dust would spoil the books.
The Long Gallery has been refilled, thanks to the V&A, with Poussin, Cuyp, Sebastiano Ricci and others. The insistence on keeping the blinds drawn makes picture-gazing here seem like swimming underwater. The swimmer must continue down the finest Adam rooms in the south wing. His early

drawing room is in deep green and gold, its ceiling roundel a burst of ostrich feathers. The furniture, the carpet, even the fire grate are all by Adam. I used to visit this room and think how well it responded to great trees waving outside. When I asked if the blind might rise to recapture this effect, I was sent on my way.

Darkness is more tolerable in the Tapestry Room next door, with its made-to-measure Gobelins to designs by Boucher. They are lit by imitation candles. Adam's exquisite ceiling, all but invisible, is reflected in the carpet, which also repeats Boucher's bunches of flowers. The bedroom beyond is dominated by a bed topped by a dome as of a Temple of Venus. It is one of Adam's most elaborate furnishings, supremely theatrical, surrounded by walls of pleated silk.

The Etruscan Dressing Room is Osterley's masterpiece, a calm celebration of the gods of love. Roman characters dance along dados, recline on platforms and lose themselves amid swirling fronds and foliage. Although Adam used the style frequently it was imitated only rarely by his contemporaries (such as Wyatt at Heaton Hall in Lancashire). Walpole regarded it as a foible, 'pure harlequinade, gingerbread and snippets of embroidery'. Today it appears serene, like a light flute playing softly. And all within a few miles of Heathrow.

Below The suite of eight carved and gilded armchairs and two sofas that stand in the Drawing Room were created by John Linnell in about 1769. The Rococo-style furniture with cabriole legs was originally upholstered in a pea-green silk damask that matched the walls of the room. The hangings were replaced in the late 19th century and the furniture recovered to match this decor in the 1970s.

Pitzhanger manor

Walpole Park, London W5; museum,
open all year

The old house at Pitzhanger was selected by Sir John Soane in 1800 as a summer retreat from his new family home in Lincoln's Inn Fields (see the Soane Museum, page 71). He also hoped that his rebuilding of it would encourage his sons to follow in his own profession. In the latter he failed. Soane never spent a night in the house, using it only for day trips out of London. He sold it within a decade.

The manor had been owned by the Gurnell family, who added a wing by the Georgian architect, George Dance. Soane demolished all except the Dance wing and rebuilt it as a variant on a classical temple. After being sold in 1810, the house was later occupied by the unmarried daughters of the murdered prime minister, Spencer Perceval, and passed to Ealing Council in 1900, reopening as a library two years later. Pitzhanger is now immaculately restored, with an art gallery attached in a 1940s extension originally built as Ealing's public library.

The front exterior has detached Ionic columns crowned by statues fronting a three-bay box. This composition is repeated pianissimo on the far side overlooking the park with pilasters similar to those on his Lincoln's Inn Fields house. The walls are in pale grey brick, lending the structure an ethereal lightness. This is a charming classical box. Dance's Georgian wing and later additions seem rather plodding next door.

The vestibule has all Soane's inventiveness. Although tiny in floor area, it soars upwards to disappear in tunnel vaults and starbursts. Medallion reliefs show the sun and moon. At the end of the vestibule, a small drawing room is on the left and the library and breakfast room run from the front to the back of the house on the right. The latter two rooms are among the most refined of their period. The library has Soane's characteristic shallow, groined-vault ceiling with coffered arches and statue niches. The ceiling has been restored with a trellis pattern.

The breakfast room is a superbly original creation. A shallow dome with clouds painted across its centre is supported by caryatid pilasters in the four corners. Walls are blue-grey and doors are inlaid with black lines, sleek and smart, like an Art Deco dressing room. These remarkable interiors come just thirty years after Adam's work and precede the voluptuous French interiors of the palaces of the Regency Court. It was a stylistic blind alley, but a sensational one.

The rest of Pitzhanger is anticlimax. The Dance extension, rightly respected by Soane, has a bold blue and white ceiling to its ground-floor dining room. The ceiling of the upstairs drawing room is of swirling Rococo arabesques above clashing Chinese wallpaper.

Below The Breakfast Room at Pitzhanger Manor is a fine example of Soane's interior decoration. The Greek-key design on his fireplace surround echoes the pattern on the domed ceiling that is picked up, in turn, in the carpet. The caryatid statues in the corners are made of Coade stone, an artificial cast material invented in the 1770s by Eleanor Coade.

Southside house

★★★ A much-altered, but much-loved, 17th-century house

Woodhayes Road, London SW19; private house, open part year

Southside is a rambling, patched and thoroughly eccentric mansion with cobwebs hanging from the ceiling and candlelit faces staring from walls. The owners are the Pennington Mellor Munthes, who are owners of the equally eccentric Hellens in Herefordshire.

The story of the present house begins with the falling of two bombs, front and back, during the Second World War. They destroyed the front hall and the rear dining room with the lady of the house, Hilda Pennington Mellor, wife of the author Axel Munthe, sheltering in the basement below. She decided to leave for Herefordshire but had no petrol or car big enough for her goods. She fled with her maid in a 100-year-old horse-drawn wagon, only to find bombs also landing on her country house. After the war, she returned to restore the building to its ancient state. Artist members of the family turned their hand to anything from a cement Baroque overmantel to ceiling murals and mock tapestries on canvas. Southside is not a work of art but something more precious, a house created and adorned by those who inhabit it.

The main front is a jumble of amendments to a Restoration core. Access is from the rear garden through a handsome Georgian doorway. Everything inside is clearly in use, although whether by a Jane Austen heroine or a Hobbit is never quite clear. Nothing quite matches anything else. An enfilade runs along the main front of the house, where everything is kept dark and candlelit. The restored

dining room rises to a pointed roof, painted sky blue. It has a Jacobean mantelpiece and is hung with 34, mostly Stuart, portraits. They include van Dycks, a Hogarth and a Burne-Jones.

The galleried entrance hall was reconstructed and repainted after the bombing. On my visit, its massive fireplace contained a huge smouldering log which filled the house with smoke and contributed further to the darkening of its surfaces. The Tapestry Room is hung with painted canvases, from which a small door gives access to a surviving powder closet. Here visitors would have their wigs re-powdered after driving across windy Wimbledon Common.

Behind is a sudden shift from Stuart dark to Georgian light. A large 18th-century music room overlooks the garden, with a screen of fluted columns and classical statues in niches. On the walls are paintings by Raeburn and Romney while against the walls are piles of old sheet music. Concerts are still held in this room, lit by candle chandeliers. Two large Chinese vases adorn one end, two of four sent by the Emperor of China to a 17th-century tsar. They 'went astray' on their journey through Asia and were acquired by a previous owner in Paris. The other two vases are apparently now in the Kremlin.

Upstairs, the house goes delightfully haywire. A library has sculpted heads of family members round the bookcases. The Prince of Wales's Room next door is the formal guest room, with a huge four-poster under a canopy and with yellow brocade wall-hangings. In this room is displayed the necklace worn by Marie Antoinette at her execution. It was removed from the scaffold and came into the possession of the young John Pennington, then serving in the British Embassy in Paris. Also to be found upstairs is a tiny chapel, surely the smallest in London, still consecrated.

Strawberry hill

★ ★ ★ Horace Walpole's Gothick fantasy

Waldegrave Road, Twickenham; private house, open part year

Horace Walpole was the younger son of England's first 'prime minister' and destined for a career in politics. From the moment he returned from the Grand Tour, he thought this an appalling idea and devoted his life to art. Apart from his diaries and letters, his one literary work was a Gothick novel, *The Castle of Otranto*. In 1747, he acquired Chopped Straw Hall, upstream of the Hanoverian court at Richmond, and rebuilt and renamed it Strawberry Hill.

Walpole's architectural fantasmagoria is now all but submerged by the adjacent St Mary's College. Whether his house is a masterpiece or merely a curiosity is a matter of opinion. In his own lifetime, it became so popular that he suggested he should marry his housekeeper, so much money was she making by charging an exorbitant guinea a visit.

Work on the new house began in 1749, with Walpole forming a Committee of Taste to assist him. Chief members were his friends Richard Bentley and John Chute. Walpole held court in

velvet and silk, with kittens and poodles littered about his feet. Friends were summoned and dismissed at will. But the outcome was the first systematic programme of Gothic Revival in England, later dubbed with a suffix -k.

The house began with the conversion of the old farm house, set on a site sloping down to the bank of the Thames. Walpole gothicized and battlemented the farm and then extended it round the garden, with a new gallery culminating in a round tower. The house remained small. To Beckford, builder of the gigantic Fonthill in Wiltshire, it was 'a Gothic mousetrap'. Even Walpole himself called it 'a little plaything house'.

The house is best entered, if possible, from the front or back door, not along the lengthy corridor from St Mary's College. The earliest rooms on either side of the entrance are cottagey, their fireplaces mostly copied from ecclesiastical tombs. Although the furniture and artefacts were dispersed after Walpole's death, efforts have been made to refurnish the rooms in his style.

The staircase was designed by Bentley after one in Rouen Cathedral. It rises to an armoury and a memorial to Walpole's much-researched but probably fake Crusader ancestor, Sir Terry Robsart. The breakfast room is like a boudoir, once containing 'a thousand plump chairs, couches and luxurious settees'. The doors and panelling are Moorish, the (later) ceiling is a fabric tent. Most successful of the earlier rooms is the library, designed by Chute. Gothick bookcases leap round the walls, culminating in a great canopy over the fireplace, copied from John of Eltham's tomb in Westminster Abbey.

Strawberry Hill now gains in confidence. The adjacent Holbein Chamber is where Walpole claimed to have had the nightmare that inspired *Otranto*. It contains Bentley's pierced screen, pinnacled fireplace and intricate ceiling, a Gothick delight by day but certainly a horror by night.

Walpole's Long Gallery is in the form of an internal cloister beneath a papier mâché fan vault. This was designed by Chute, Bentley having now been discarded because his wife was judged unable to behave 'with people of the first rank'. The gallery is flanked by Gothick canopies hiding vaulted alcoves and mirrors. I encountered an American lady photographing them in minute detail, 'to give to my interior decorator back home'.

Of the remaining rooms, the Tribune copies its roof from the Chapter House at York, its ribs and vaults like swirling flames. The Round Room (designed by Robert Adam no less) takes its chimneypiece from Edward the Confessor's tomb at Westminster. The ceiling is based on the rose window in Old St Paul's. A frieze of tiny acanthus leaves is Adam's only apparent signature.

Syon house

★★★★★ Historic noble house with sublime Robert Adam interiors

Syon Park, Brentford; private house, open part year

Syon House is phenomenal, an aristocratic seat complete with private estate, park and river frontage inside the boundaries of London. The family is the Percys, Earls then Dukes of Northumberland, to whom the former monastic property of Syon passed in 1597. The Percys were architecturally conservative. They never replaced the old house, rather converting it gradually over the generations.

Adam's work at Syon dates from 1761, three years after his return from Italy and already fiercely ambitious. The Northumberland commission was a valuable catch. The Percy heiress, Elizabeth Seymour, had married the progressive and energetic Sir Hugh Smithson who, in 1750, became Earl, later 1st Duke, of Northumberland. He told Adam to leave the exterior alone. Adam duly treated the castellated exterior as a disguise for the splendours within. Only two pavilions in the grounds and the Adam gate on the main road suggest this is a house of the 18th century. The latter carries the Percy lion, moved from the demolished Northumberland House in London's Strand.

The front door opens directly on the Great Hall. This serene chamber is the Georgian ideal of a Roman senate house. The cross-beams of the ceiling, coated in plaster anthemions, are reflected in the chequered marble floor. Figures of Greek and Roman dignitaries line the walls. Screens at each end flank steps to the reception rooms beyond. In front of these screens are copies of two famous statues of antiquity, the *Dying Gaul* and the *Apollo Belvedere*.

'Adam treated the castellated exterior as a disguise for the splendours within.'

Above The ceiling and gilded wall panels in the superb ante room are by the famous stuccoist, Joseph Rose. Robert Adam was reported to have been so delighted with Rose's work here that he paid him out of his own pocket. The gilded statues of classical figures that stand above each of the scagliola columns were made by John Cheere.

Next comes the ante room, among the most sumptuous classical chambers in England. Adam turned a simple cube into a temple of marble and gold. To Sacheverell Sitwell it was 'as superb as any Roman interior in the palace of the Caesars'. Twelve columns allegedly dredged from the bed of the Tiber were acquired for £1,000 apiece and coated in scagliola. Their entablature occupies the entire top third of the room. Gilded statues from antiquity are interspersed with panels of gold on green. Ceiling echoes floor and floor ceiling.

The ante-room turns the corner of the house to be followed by the quieter dining room. Here is another demonstration of Adam's skill at expanding a small space to create a big one, by means of niches, screens, apses and perspective. The chimneypiece is by Joseph Rose and depicts the *Three Graces*. Rose also executed the abstract pattern of the ceiling.

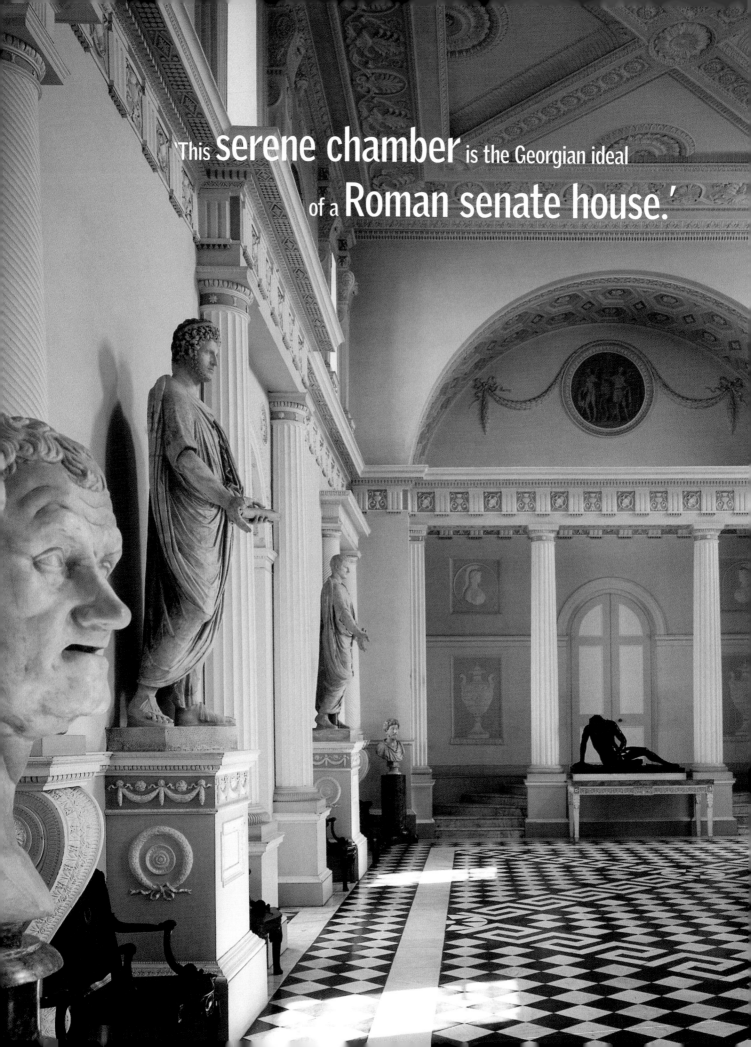

'This **serene chamber** is the Georgian ideal of a **Roman senate house**.'

Left Robert Adam was instructed 'to create a palace of Graeco-Roman splendour' at Syon. Probably inspired by Piranesi, he based the Great Hall on a Roman basilica. The 1st Duke and Duchess of Northumberland furnished the room with suitable classical statues. In 1773 they paid £300 for a copy by Luigi Valadier of the *Dying Gaul*. The bronze had been cast in Rome and then left immersed in water for nine years to give it the right patina.

After the relative calm of the dining room, the Red Drawing Room returns to full throttle. Walls are hung with faded crimson silk, offsetting the brilliant gold of the ceiling, where a kaleidoscope of classical medallions by Cipriani coats the surface. The doorcases are of gold leaf on ivory. The room has tables of mosaic, one with a top from the Baths of Titus, and a Georgian cylinder bureau covered in marquetry. On the walls are Stuart portraits, including Lely's Charles I with his son, James, and a van Dyck of Queen Henrietta Maria.

Adam planned the Long Gallery as a drawing room for ladies, to separate them from the male noise of the dining room. He took the Elizabethan gallery, which would have been a long, monotonous chamber, and gave rhythm to its walls and ceiling. Pilasters are spaced to make it seem both longer and wider. Doors, fireplaces and niches are all pressed to this purpose, as are the diagonal patterns in the ceiling. The room is decorated in pinks and mauves, softening the gilding and making the books and Percy medallions seem like precious objects attached to the walls.

The room culminates in a tiny pink-and-blue domed closet, a conversation piece in which a mechanical bird is invited to join. From the windows the view is completely rural, over the water meadows to the banks of the Thames and the great trees of Kew.

After these rooms, Syon becomes just another country house. Rooms are enlivened by Adam fittings imported from Northumberland House. Syon's gardens are partly private, but the great conservatory and arboretum are accessible.

Whitehall

⭐ Tudor timber-framed house with clapboard exterior

Malden Road, Cheam; museum, open all year

If someone had the courage to grab the centre of Cheam by the throat, demolish what is ugly and fill in the gaps, it would be a jewel of South London. A scatter of old houses survives across Malden Road to the west of the church, clapboarded and painted like a New England township. Pride of place goes to Whitehall. Begun *c*1500 and immaculately restored by Sutton Council, the only sadness is that its two chief rooms, the hall and parlour, are shops.

The exterior is charming. White clapboards cover a timber frame, parts of which can still be seen in the wall of the rear kitchen. The door has a porch tower over it, while the wings are jettied both front and back. The old hall was not open to its roof but two-storeyed and chimneyed from the start, a thoroughly modern Tudor property. The house belonged in the 17th century to a local clergyman, who added a wing to the back. It was bought by the Killick family in the 18th century, who sold it to the local council in 1963.

The interiors suffer museumitis, but fireplaces and beams remain and the floors retain a satisfactory creak. A Cheam schoolmaster's study bedroom has been re-created in the attic, in all its cluttered asceticism. Three masters once lived here. To the rear an early garden has been re-created.

2 Willow road

★ Modernist home of the 1930s

Willow Road, London NW3; National Trust, open part year

Ask not the reason why. After the death in 1987 of the Austrian-Hungarian architect, Ernö Goldfinger, his acolytes pleaded for the National Trust to buy and preserve his house and its contents. This was done in 1994. The property is outwardly (and inwardly) unremarkable, a rectangular box of three small houses built by Goldfinger after coming to London in 1934. He occupied the largest, middle one. Here, at least, was a Modern Movement house in which its architect lived.

The building attracted outrage when constructed in 1937. Pevsner had to defend it vigorously as 'the contemporary style in an uncompromising form', that is of three storeys 'of reinforced concrete, with columns exposed on the ground floor, and with concrete used also for framing the openings in the brick-faced walls'. The brick facing makes it early Goldfinger. Later it would have been all concrete.

The guidebook says that Goldfinger was eager to display his talents to his new English parents-in-law, who were heirs to the Crosse and Blackwell fortune. The house is small but was given 'servants' quarters' in the basement and garaging for two cars, one with an inspection pit. The interior is consistent with the exterior. The entrance lobby, cramped by the garage, leads up a spindly spiral staircase to a living, dining and study floor, more or less open plan. Furnishings are spare and vaguely Scandinavian. There is little sense of privacy. The first floor is an uninterrupted expanse of glass, front and back, offering fine views of Hampstead Heath.

The one relief is the warm parquet flooring and liberal use of panelling. Shelves, dividers, chairs and tables are mostly by Goldfinger. The dining table is topped in lino, chairs are made of plywood and such materials as tubular steel and Bakelite are much in evidence. Anatomical studies by Goldfinger's wife, Ursula, decorate the walls, alongside works by Max Ernst, Bridget Riley and Henry Moore.

Left Goldfinger's interiors at Willow Road are as Modernist as the exterior (above), and intended to maximize the use of limited space. Folding doors, the full width of the room, open to join the architect's studio to the living room beyond, forming one large room that culminates in floor-to-ceiling glass doors onto the balcony.

Surrey

Claremont

Surrey

Clandon park

★★★ Palladian mansion with 19th-century *porte-cochère*

At West Clandon, 3 miles E of Guildford; National Trust, open part year

Onslows were lawyers. Three rose to be Speakers of the House of Commons, the first being 'Black Onslow' in the reign of Elizabeth I. The family acquired the Clandon estate in 1641 and continued in the style of their profession, steering a course between Royalty and Revolution, corruption and integrity, high office and high dudgeon. Onslows regarded the Lord Lieutenancy of Surrey as a hereditary right. In 1813, eight Onslows were county JPs. The family built a new mansion at Clandon c1731. The house experienced the familiar saga of brilliance, decline, ruin and rescue. In 1956 the family passed the house to the National Trust whilst continuing to live in a house in the park.

Clandon is indeed a lawyer of a house, formal to the world behind a Victorian porch, but with a certain pompous jollity in private. The designer was the Venetian, Giacomo Leoni, builder of Lyme Park in Cheshire. His client, the 2nd Baron Onslow, had profited hugely from his marriage to a Jamaica heiress, Elizabeth Knight. She was said to be so miserable that her ghost still haunts the house. I once visited

Above The magnificent stucco decoration in the Marble Hall was by Giuseppe Artari and Giovanni Bagutti, who also created the plasterwork at Orleans House Octogan (see page 144). The sculptor Michael Rysbrack depicted sacrifices in the chimneypiece reliefs – one associated with the goddess Diana, the other with Bacchus, Roman god of wine.

Clandon with its windows still shuttered. The parade of gloomy rooms overseen by portraits of dark, domineering Onslows was a good place for such a ghost.

The house includes one of the great rooms of early Georgian England, the Marble Hall. Unlike the house of Onslow's rival, Walpole's Houghton Hall in Norfolk, Clandon permits access directly into the Great Hall. The effect is sensational. White and dazzling, the walls rise through two storeys of orders past balconies to a spectacular ceiling. This might be an Italian *cortile* with the mythical gods romping across the *trompe-l'œil* sky above. The stuccoists, Giuseppe Artari and Giovanni Bagutti, have here bettered their ceiling at Houghton. Putti and slaves are in deep relief, their legs and arms hanging free yet foreshortened as they spill over the coving into space. The chimneypieces are by Rysbrack. The room is further enlivened by two pictures of an ostrich and a cassowary, by Francis Barlow.

The rooms at Clandon are heavily classical, so much as to be almost relentless. They are relieved by the light touch of Artari and Bagutti, notably the ceilings of the Palladian Room and the saloon. Relief is also supplied by Clandon's other treasure, the collection of furniture and porcelain gathered between the wars by Mrs David Gubbay and donated to the National Trust. It was allocated to Clandon to replace much that had been sold, an admirable partnership.

While the Gubbay furniture seems to merge into the background of the rooms, the porcelain is a different matter. It includes some fifty Chinese birds, which seem to flutter from every mantelpiece. They are everywhere, perching on top of cabinets and side tables and darting among the Meissen, Sèvres and Bow. They bring colour when it is needed and delicacy when the ponderous Onslows seem overpowering.

Of the individual reception rooms, the Hunting Room contains a set of Soho tapestries to designs by Wootton. The Speakers' Room is dedicated to the three Onslows who attained that office. The Stone Staircase is hung with paintings of racehorses by Ferneley.

Claremont

Catch Claremont in a good light and it might still be shimmering in a landscape in India. It was bought by Lord Clive in 1769, after his return from India, to complement his sumptuous house in Berkeley Square. The house was originally built by Vanbrugh as his own, on a sight looking over Surrey towards London. Vanbrugh sold it to the Duke of Newcastle in 1714, who enlarged it to the size seen today. Clive brought in Capability Brown to redesign the house and landscape; Brown employed his son-in-law, Henry Holland, on the interiors and Holland in turn collaborated with the young John Soane. The mansion dominates Brown's sweeping park. Vanbrugh is recalled only by a belvedere on an adjacent knoll, although his original walled garden still exists nearby.

The house is now an independent school. As John Julius Norwich wrote, we can only feel for the pupils 'who, on the first evening of their first term, climb the twenty-two steps to that gigantic portico'. The house is a box of white brick with stone dressings. The front portico is of four giant Corinthian columns, the back has pilasters. The coat of arms includes an elephant and a griffin. While the front steps are straight, those behind are beautifully curved. Here, Clive can have imagined himself still a proconsul, ruling Esher as if it were Madras.

The house was advanced. The basement was designed to ensure that servants did not suffer damp. Clive also insisted on a separate underground block housing the kitchen, water closets and a vaulted bathroom big enough for swimming. He committed suicide in 1774 before he was able to enjoy any of this.

The interior is very much a school, but this in no way detracts from its majesty. The entrance hall is an oval of red scagliola columns inside a rectangle, a design for which Soane was later to claim credit. The ceiling is reflected in the pattern of the marble floor. On the walls are reliefs of Victory apparently resting on her laurels and surrounded by trophies.

The former reception rooms were decorated by Holland, with fine ceilings and Adamish motifs on the doors and cornices. Some of the designs he went on to use at Berrington Hall, Herefordshire, on a more intimate scale. In 1816, the government acquired Claremont for the Prince Regent's daughter and her husband, the future King of the Belgians. The young Victoria often stayed in the house and worshipped in the private pew that Vanbrugh designed in Esher church.

Some 50 acres of grounds laid out by Vanbrugh, Bridgeman and Kent are now run by the National Trust. Brown's belong to the school.

Farnham castle

★★ Keep and former house of the Bishops of Winchester

At Farnham, 8 miles W of Guildford; private house, open all year

The castle sits high on its bluff over the town as if Surrey were the Dordogne. It belonged to the Bishops of Winchester, a stopping place on the way to and from London and close to the Pilgrims' Way. The keep dates from the 12th century, as does the triangular bailey immediately below it, with curtain wall immediately beneath. The keep (owned by English Heritage) is merely a bastion, offering a good view of the North Downs. The bailey embraces a remarkable range of old buildings, now an international business college.

The plan of the domestic quarters can be seen from the inner courtyard. A Great Hall faced the entrance, with the old chapel to its right and kitchens behind. Farther round are Tudor guest rooms behind timbered walls. The bishop's lodgings were to the left. The whole castle was badly mauled during the Civil War, but it was rebuilt after the Restoration by Bishop George Morley, to whom we owe most of the present residence.

His hall is a large Carolean chamber rising two storeys and with balconies on two sides. Its fireplace is truly episcopal, flanked by giant consoles instead of pilasters. The balcony and upper rooms are reached by a magnificent staircase, showing a mastery of architectural space. The fruit-covered newel posts were reputedly by Grinling Gibbons, as are the swags and drops of Morley's upstairs chapel. The remaining rooms are institutional. The drawing room is said to have a fine scissorbeam roof hidden above its ceiling.

On the other side of the hall is some surviving medieval work. Fox's Tower, built by Bishop Waynflete in the 1470s, dominates the town below. Beyond are Norman kitchens with a large fireplace. Next to them is a Norman chapel, still consecrated for services.

Godalming: Red house

★ Edwin Lutyens house, overlooking a wooded Surrey valley

Frith Hill Road, Godalming, 4 miles SW of Guildford; private house

This eccentric house is strictly for Lutyens addicts. The architect designed it when he was just twenty-eight and on the brink of celebrity. It clings to the edge of a precipice, as might an early work by Frank Lloyd Wright. Round it slope the remains of Gertrude Jekyll's attempt at mountain gardening. The house was built for a master at Charterhouse, W. H. Evans, in 1897 (the view shown is from Charterhouse grounds). The fall of land appealed to the theatrical in Lutyens.

The house is modestly neo-Georgian to the road above, marked only by massive Lutyens chimneys. From here it might be a two-storey town house. The more remarkable elevation is overlooking the valley below, a bold wall of plain brick with canted bays and casement windows. It harks back to Elizabethan Hardwick Hall in Derbyshire and forward to Lutyens's own Castle Drogo in Devon.

Inside, the spaces are dictated not by a hall but by a wide spiral staircase, running up the core of the house, much of which is below the level of the entrance. The treads are wide and shallow, to accommodate the disablement of the original owner. The staircase is now the best thing left of the interior, apart from two Lutyens fireplaces with niches.

The current owner is struggling to bring the rooms back to their original appearance. He has a long way to go. Jekyll's garden seems beyond recall.

Great Fosters

★ ★ Tudor house with Jacobean interiors

At Egham, 1 mile SW of Staines; now a hotel

Great Fosters dates from the 1550s and was reputedly used by Elizabeth I as a hunting lodge. Its most intriguing occupant was Sir John Chapman, a progressive doctor who was said to have treated George III for his madness in Windsor. Rumour, though not record, even has the King being brought to Great Fosters in person for treatment. The house was modernized by the up-market country house architect, W. H. Romaine-Walker, after 1918. It is a rare and surprisingly little-known Elizabethan house so close to London.

Above Great Fosters could be described as the first truly grand country-house hotel. In keeping with that role, the bedrooms are decorated in lavish style. In the Italian bedroom a pair of quattrocento doors, heavy with intricate plasterwork, dominate one of the damask-lined walls. Suitable antiques and artefacts have been imported into the room to complete the impression of old-world oppulence.

Since 1930, the Sutcliffe family have run Great Fosters as a discreet hotel, convenient for Ascot. It hosted the Ascot Ball in 1931, with royalty present. The appearance is still that of a private house at which guests would arrive only if invited. There is a wicket gate in the front door.

The main entrance carries the date of 1598, but the hall beams are older. The Jacobean fireplace must have contributed to the thick yellow patina on the plaster ceiling. The original staircase survives behind the hall in a rear turret. The stair baluster is heavy and crude, with a giant newel post rising to the ceiling. This contrasts with the staircase's later and more delicate wall panelling.

The old drawing room, now the (Flemish) Tapestry Room, has a Jacobean chimneypiece depicting the story of Genesis. The Anne Boleyn Room retains its original ceiling. It is decorated with emblems of the queen, whether in her honour or because of a claimed link with the house is unknown. The garden dates from the 1918 redesign and includes fine topiary, a knot garden and an early swimming pool with 'listed' bathing boxes. The tithe barn is extraordinarily old, and is dated 1390; it was moved here from Ewell.

Abbot's hospital

High Street, Guildford; private house, open for tours by arrangement

The grandest building in Guildford High Street is not a town hall, church or hotel. It is the gatehouse of the Hospital of the Blessed Trinity. Access is by friendly appointment, through a gigantic door panelled with heraldry and topped by a wooden Gothic fan light.

George Abbot was a Guildford man who rose from humble origins to be Archbishop of Canterbury in the troubled early 17th century. His brothers became Bishop of Salisbury and Lord Mayor of London, sign of the upward mobility of late-Tudor England. In 1619 Abbot founded an almshouse in the town 'out of my love to the place of my birth'. It opened in 1622, housing twelve brothers and eight sisters. They had to live in the town, be over 60 and of good character. There are twenty-six residents today.

The gatehouse is that of a traditional Jacobean building, strongly built as if for defence. The main reception rooms are above the entrance, in a century-old fashion familiar from Layer Marney, in Essex, and Oxburgh Hall, in Norfolk. The quadrangle has two storeys with an attic, all redbrick, and might be the court of a Cambridge college. The whole building seems a deliberate anachronism, as if so elevated a purpose demanded a medieval form.

The communal interiors can be visited. The Common Hall is beautifully panelled and furnished with old settles, simple but comfortable. The Guesten Hall has a Jacobean overmantel with grotesque carvings and portraits of donors. Doors and hinges are superbly crafted.

Left A wicket door in the gatehouse opens onto the hospital quadrangle.

GUILDFORD

Guildford house

⭐ 17th-century townhouse with original plasterwork

High Street, Guildford; museum, open all year

GUILDFORD

Despite the ugliness of Guildford below the hill, the old High Street displays the best of Surrey townscape. Its jolliest building is this Restoration town house. Although the ground floor was long ago converted to a shopfront, the upper storeys are a spirited work of 1660. The house was built by a lawyer, John Child, and later sold to a mayor of Guildford, John Martyr. It became the local museum in the 1950s.

The façade above the ground floor might be termed 'Inigo Jones provincial'. The façade is almost all window, with the upper floors jettied over the pavement. Yet the casements are divided by four bold pilasters rising to an overhanging entablature, the middle two bays slightly projected, a most inventive composition. A 17th-century balcony overlooks the street from above the front door. The rear is equally enjoyable, tile hung and with a pretty oriel window.

The interior is mostly spoilt by museum use, the walls frigidly white with little feeling of the old house. But the staircase survives, a generous structure with original pattern of acanthus leaves for its balustrade. The newel posts carry urns of flowers. The Powell Room on the first floor has an original plaster ceiling of circles and ovals divided by ornamented beams. The survival of the casement windows and their old handles is particularly happy.

Hatchlands park

✫ ✫ ✫ Robert Adam house, home to the Cobbe Collection or artefacts and musical instruments

Near East Clandon, 4 miles E of Guildford; National Trust, open part year

Hatchlands is a jewel in the National Trust crown. This is due to its having the collector, Alec Cobbe, as its tenant and giving him freedom to furnish an empty house to his own, sometimes controversial, taste. A shell left to the Trust in 1945 by the architect, H. S. Goodhart-Rendel, is now filled with pictures, furniture and historic keyboard instruments. Some were moved from Cobbe's family house outside Dublin. His particular delight is to wander the rooms with visitors, stopping at an instrument and playing snatches of music.

The house, begun in the 1750s by a sea captain, Admiral Boscawen, was built like Thomas Anson's Shugborough on the spoils of Georgian piracy. He commissioned Stiff Leadbetter to design the unexciting exterior and the young Robert Adam, then just back from Italy, on the far more exciting interior. Repton arrived later to lay out the park. Like the adjacent Clandon, Hatchlands retains open Surrey countryside within its borders.

Adam reigns supreme, but it is an unfamiliar, youthful Adam. The date is 1758–9 and the classical detail is relatively heavy, closer to the earlier Georgian of Leoni at Clandon. In addition, the Adam work was so battered after the war that Cobbe, himself a painter, has reinstated much of it to his own researched designs. The library has an Adam ceiling and cornice, with roundels by Cobbe 'after' Angelica Kauffmann.

The adjacent saloon is hung with red silk beneath a spectacular Adam ceiling of swirling acanthus. The frieze, celebrating

Above The Saloon was intended to be the Great Dining Room in Admiral Boscawen's original house. Today, it contains a pair of gilt console tables with eagle supports, *c*1740, that are the most important pieces of furniture to have survived from Boscawen's time at Hatchlands. When Alec Cobbe became the tenant, in 1987, the room was decorated with red silk to provide a suitably traditional background for his Old-Masters collection.

Boscawen's maritime career, is of dolphins, similar to those on Adam's Admiralty Screen in Whitehall. The fireplace, flanked by two giant caryatids, was carved by Rysbrack. This saloon is the principal exhibition room of the house, hung with Old Masters from the Cobbe collection and dominated by a Guercino. These are interspersed with family portraits, Cobbe claiming descent from both Cromwell and Charles II through the Duchess of Cleveland. The room could be in a Venetian palazzo.

Apart from pictures, the rooms are crammed with keyboard instruments. Everywhere are pianos, some fifty slotted into every alcove and corner. Each has a story and a personality of its own. There are pianos owned by Beethoven, by Marie Antoinette, by the Medici and one played by Mozart. Each seems eager to vanish beneath the clutter, as if to avoid another Cobbe performance. This is erudite clutter, in blessed contrast to customary National Trust tidiness. Music and books are stacked on chairs and side tables. The artful mind cannot be neat.

The staircase hall soars the full height of the house, making it seem higher than it is. It was embellished *c*1800, probably by Bonomi. An alcove below contains Mahler's piano. Beyond is the Edwardian music room, added by Sir Reginald Blomfield. It offers eight more pianos, including ones played by Liszt and Chopin and that on which Elgar composed the Enigma Variations.

In the dining room, a sideboard lid opens to reveal yet another piano. This is a house as it should be, occupied, loved and nudged this way and that by its inhabitant – and to hell with the owner.

'... closed to envy
but **open always**
to a **friend.'**

Right The Great Hall is packed with portraits. Full-length paintings by John de Critz of James I and his Queen, Anne of Denmark, hang on the south wall; they were presented to Loseley by the King himself. A portrait of Edward VI hangs beside the fire. Most of the other paintings are of the More-Molyneux family and their ancestors. A large group portrait, actually painted in the Hall in 1739, shows Sir More Molyneux, his wife Cassandra, and eight of their eleven children.

Loseley was one of the earliest houses to open to the public after the war. Its motto claims, 'I am closed to envy but open always to a friend.' The owners, Mr and Mrs More-Molyneux, recall that the place was transformed overnight from somewhere 'grubby, geriatric, unkempt, into a beautiful creature, friendly, steeped in peace, that people loved to visit'. Owners were as pleased as was the public.

Loseley was built by an Elizabethan courtier, Sir William More, who added to an earlier house in 1562. It was intended, like so many mansions at the time, to entertain the Queen on her progress round the country, yet in the hope that she would not bring bankruptcy in her train. She visited Loseley in 1570 and the house survived. A More heiress married Sir Thomas Molyneux and inherited the house in 1689. The house has been owned by More-Molyneuxs ever since.

This is now a house, a home and very much a business. All seem in good health. As in Elizabethan days, the family are preoccupied with hospitality. The house is set in a spacious

Loseley park

★ ★ ★ Tudor family house, once favoured with royal visits

2 miles SW of Guildford; private house, open part year

park, home to the celebrated Loseley herd of dairy cattle and the resulting dairy products. The exterior appears at first glance a typical Tudor E-plan, of white stone rubble. It is asymmetrical, with windows still reflecting the internal plan in the medieval style. The entrance bay is off-centre and narrow. The Great Hall has a wide bay window.

Inside, this is a magnificent room. The panelling was allegedly imported from the demolished Nonsuch Palace, an attribution based on emblems of Henry VIII and Katherine Parr. The painted canvas panels in the gallery are from Henry's banqueting tents, of high quality and great rarity. The designs are Italian, remarkable for their date in England. The screen doors have elaborate *trompe-l'œil* marquetry.

Beyond the Great Hall is the library, a rich chamber with pilastered bookcases and a cornice carrying the maxim, 'I soothe troubled minds and while away the centuries'. Over the eccentric mantelpiece, which seems a Victorian amalgam, is a panel commemorating the coveted visit by Elizabeth I.

An even more elaborate ceiling with pendants graces the remarkable drawing room, apparently inserted for a visit from James I. Its mantelpiece is carved from a single block of chalk, a mass of swirling scrollwork inside a classical frame, guarded by caryatids and monsters. The Mannerist style is wayward and enjoyable. So too is the huge Mannerist mullion to the window, ending in a giant claw. It must be something that a Tudor mason saw in an Italian pattern book.

Upstairs three bedrooms are displayed, all with geometrical ribbed ceilings and stately panelling. Two contain spectacular 17th-century Oudenarde tapestries. One set depicts a hunt at night and is said to come to life if lit with a red light after dark.

Nonsuch mansion house

★ ☆ Gothick house by Wyatville in the grounds of a lost palace

At Cheam, 1 mile W of Sutton; private house (view by arrangement); museum, open part year

The demolition of Henry VIII's palace of Nonsuch, or 'Nonpareil', was one of the catastrophes of English architecture. Towards the end of his life and as its crowning glory, Henry brought artists and craftsmen from all over Europe to demonstrate Tudor England's Renaissance prowess. What had begun as a royal hunting lodge emerged as an English Fontainebleau. The palace was so famous that it was depicted throughout the land on so-called 'Nonsuch' chests. After Henry's death, Elizabeth visited the house but it was eventually given to the grandson of the Duchess of Cleveland. He could not afford it and demolition began in the 1680s. Only a few outbuildings survived.

Nonsuch Park, which straddles the London boundary at Cheam, is picturesque. Fragments of Elizabethan wall abound. Fine oak avenues have been planted and the undulating terrain retains a sense of its hunting past. The old quarry has been converted into a dell. The site of the palace, in the south-west corner of the park, was inexcusably covered after excavation in 1959. The adjacent Cherry Orchard farm survives.

One outbuilding to the north-east was said to have belonged to a palace official with the title of 'the Sergeant of the Sauces'. This passed in 1799 to Samuel Farmer of Cheshire. He commissioned a new building on the site in Tudor Gothic style from Sir Jeffry Wyatville; it was begun in 1802. Whether Wyatville sought to imitate the original façade of Nonsuch can only be a matter of conjecture.

Nonsuch Mansion House has its own garden, parterre and copse of trees and is a substantial Gothic building. It passed from the Farmers, who rose to be Lords Lieutenant of Surrey, to the local council in 1937 and has been well restored.

Wyatville's house survives virtually unaltered. The exterior has tall Gothick windows, turrets and a battlemented roof. Gothick woodwork and plasterwork are intact in the main reception rooms, including doors and window shutters. The interiors have been restored to their original colours. Many are similar to Wyatville's later work at Windsor Castle.

Thus the entrance hall is dark brown, with shields picked out in the frieze. The library and drawing room run together from front to back, with ceilings of unusual richness. Niches for pier-glasses are uniformly Gothic. The windows have Victorian stained glass depicting Henry VIII and Elizabeth I, and a Tudor rose decorates the dining room ceiling. Such echoes of Nonsuch are repeated throughout the house, interspersed with the Farmer coat of arms.

The Friends of Nonsuch battled in 1992 to prevent the house and park becoming a golf club. They are restoring the Georgian service wing, which survives from a precursor of the Wyatville house, reinstating the scullery, game store, kitchens and laundry. On display is a set of Nonsuch glass, including a 'parakeet' work of stained glass painted by Margaret Pearson in 1776.

Polesden Lacey

 Regency villa with Edwardian interiors

Near Great Bookham, 5 miles NW of Dorking; National Trust, open part year

The defining event in the history of Polesden Lacey was its purchase by Mr and Mrs Ronald Greville in 1906. Mrs Greville, heiress to the Scottish McEwen's brewery fortune, converted the house into a place of lavish and apparently majestic entertainment.

She was a social monster: 'better a beeress than a peeress,' she said. To Balfour, her acerbic wit was 'honeyed poison'. To Cecil Beaton she was a 'galumphing, greedy, snobbish old toad'. She went to the Nuremberg rally and supported the fascists as 'better than the bolshies'. Yet she was hugely hospitable and her food and wine were superb. Kings and prime ministers found themselves swept into her circle. Edward VII, an expert at being entertained, described her 'gift for hospitality' as amounting to 'positive genius'. On her death in 1942, Mrs Greville left the house, park and art collection to the nation.

The house had previously been occupied until his death in 1816 by the playwright Richard Brinsley Sheridan. It was then largely demolished and rebuilt by Thomas Cubitt, builder of Belgravia. The 1821 exterior is that of a neo-classical seaside villa, well set on the edge of a steep slope and park. Surrey is a place of many secrets.

On buying the house, Mrs Greville employed the Ritz architects, Mewès and Davis, to convert the interiors for entertainment. Her husband, a self-effacing Tory MP, died within two years of their

taking up residence, but this only increased his wife's social activity, both here and at her house in Charles Street, Mayfair. She revelled in her ability to attract nobility to her table and once boasted that three kings had sat on her bed at her morning levée. The late Queen Mother began her honeymoon at Polesden in 1923.

The house carries its opulence with an intimacy rare in Edwardian interiors. The central hall is spacious, adorned with a magnificent reredos from Wren's church of St Matthew's, Friday Street in the City. The dining room is hung with British portraits by Lawrence, Reynolds and Raeburn. In this room occurred the most celebrated Greville anecdote. Alarmed at the state of her butler, she passed him a note telling him he was drunk and should leave at once. The butler duly passed the note to the principal guest, the Tory grandee Sir Austen Chamberlain. The under-butler was an overt Communist.

The barrel-vaulted corridor has a Jacobean-style ceiling. With plaster scrollwork, dark panelling and red carpet, it is a perfect setting for works by de Hooch, Teniers, Cuyp and van Goyen. Indeed Polesden houses one of the Trust's finest if little known collections. At the end of the corridor is a portrait by Carolus-Duran of a more than life-size Mrs Greville, looking improbably demure at the time of her marriage.

The library is kept full of flowers from the garden. Beyond is Mrs Greville's study, with her collection of Meissen and a Fürstenberg tea-caddy decorated with oriental scenes. The saloon was Mewès and Davis at their most Ritzy: 'fit to entertain maharajahs in' was the instruction. To Beverley Nichols, from a later and no less snobbish generation, it was 'over-gilt, over-velveted, over-mirrored like an extremely expensive bordel'. The National Trust plans to permit billiards in the billiard room, a good innovation. Next they should permit cigars in the smoking room.

Above left A portrait of Mrs Greville by the French artist Carolus-Duran. The painting dominates one end of the barrel-vaulted corridor that links the ground floor rooms at Polesden Lacey. **Above right** The panelled walls of the corridor are hung with artworks from Mrs Greville's extensive collection. **Above centre** Mrs Greville's presence is everywhere. The Tea Room is arranged as it would have been in her day, with tables set for afternoon tea. One guest, Beverley Nichols, described Mrs Greville's tea table as 'rich in charming detail', laid with Queen Anne silver, Meissen porcelain and monogrammed Chantilly lace. Osbert Sitwell said of Polesden hospitality that it was an 'unobtrusive luxury of life ... never encountered elsewhere'. **Right** A stone griffin looks out from Polesden Lacey's grounds over the rolling North Downs.

Royal Holloway college

Like it or loathe it, the Royal Holloway is a phenomenon without equal. To some it suggests a creation of the cartoonist, Charles Addams. From a distance, including from the M25, the place shimmers above the tree-line like a lost temple in the Cambodian jungle.

The college was built by Thomas Holloway with the millions that he made from 'Holloway's Patent Pills'. He was an epic Victorian entrepreneur/philanthropist, his wife a passionate believer in women's education. Holloway created what must have been the largest single building in England and filled it with young ladies and with art. Apart from the addition of some male students, it remains true to his principles to this day.

The building itself was erected in just eight years from 1879. Holloway's template was the Château de Chambord on the Loire. His architect, W. H. Crossland, was sent for two years to study the château before beginning work. The result is a variation on a French Renaissance theme, a monumental house blown up by three, four, five times the normal size round two spacious courtyards,

yet its scale is not relentless or even institutional. Crossland achieved a careful sense of proportion and covered it in ornamental detail. Like Sir Gilbert Scott's St Pancras Chambers, this is a Victorian building that can handle its size. I am not sure we can.

The building is near impossible to describe in detail. Three gatehouses penetrate the two courtyards, as in St John's College, Cambridge. The exterior is adorned with projecting turrets every few bays, rising to towers (or tourelles). These are interspersed with chimneys adorned with segmental pediments and a parade of dormers. The courtyards carry Renaissance frontispieces left and right, with colonnades along the main façades. The central lanterns are elaborate coronets, the middle one with giant crocodiles climbing up its buttresses. In one court is a statue of Queen Victoria, in the other Holloway and his wife, portrayed as assisting the cause of education.

The interiors are by contrast dull, although the chapel has a magnificent Renaissance roof. The figures in its frieze are in deep relief, as if about to pounce on the girls below. In the Picture Gallery is Holloway's collection of Victorian art. This includes such celebrated works as Frith's *Paddington Station* and Luke Fildes' *Applicants for Admission to a Casual Ward*.

Titsey place

⋆⋆ Regency house overlooking a North Downs estate

2 miles NW of Oxted; private house, open part year

Five miles south of Croydon, London runs into the rolling foothills of the North Downs. Suburb retreats and thickly wooded slopes lead towards the steep southern escarpment, with views over the Weald. Hidden along this escarpment is the old Leveson Gower estate. For a brief moment, we might be in Gloucestershire.

Titsey was one of the many properties of the Elizabethan Gresham family, City merchants and builders of Osterley Park (see page 146). The line descended through daughters to the Leveson Gowers (pronounced Looson Gores). By the 20th century they found themselves with three bachelor brothers and, in 1992, no heirs. The estate, one of the largest in Surrey, passed to a trust in the care of David Innes, godson of one of the brothers. He occupies the house and opens it and its grounds to the public.

After a drive across sweeping grassland, past cedars and Wellingtonias, the house presents a pale face to the world. It was the work in 1826 of James Wyatt's assistant, William Atkinson, in neo-Tudor with grey render. The exterior encases a Georgian predecessor, built by Sir John Gresham in 1775, and this in turn encases a Tudor original round what is now a servants' hall. This is a house of many boxes.

The character of Titsey largely rests with the genealogy-obsessed Squire Granville Leveson Gower. Between 1860 and 1895, he built cottages, lodges and a church on the estate and planted half a million trees. He added a large battlemented tower to the north side of the house, destroying the symmetry of Atkinson's Regency façade. The inside he filled with Leveson Gower portraits, coats of arms and antiques. Excellent panelling was imported from elsewhere. One such piece is the 1646 chimney surround in the drawing room.

The rather ordinary interior is redeemed by the care of the restoration to Squire Granville's period. Thus Atkinson's staircase landing is lit by a skylight crowded with heraldic glass. The boudoir, over the Victorian dining room below, contains a collection of 16th and 17th-century panelling, gathered by the Squire. It is offset by a fireplace surrounded with Delftware tiles. The dining room has four lovely Canalettos of Venice and in the Old Dining Room hangs a portrait of the last Leveson Gower brothers, by the wildlife artist, David Shepherd.

Glossary

The aim in this book has been to avoid terms not familiar to the lay person. However, some specialist terms in common use in architectural circles may have crept in, for which the following may be helpful.

acanthus – pattern of an exotic Mediterranean flower with large leaves used in classical decoration.

anthemion – a honeysuckle flower pattern used in classical decoration.

Artisan Mannerist – buildings created by masons using pattern books (rather than architects) in the period c.1615–75. Mannerism originated in 16th-century Italy and was characterised by Classical elements used in unusual ways. It was taken up in the Low Countries, then spread to England.

ashlar – any block of masonry fashioned into a wall, either load-bearing or covering brick.

bailey, inner and outer – a fortified enclosure, usually moated and surrounded by a curtain wall, containing a motte (mound) on which stands a keep. Walls are topped by battlements, with crenellations which protected defenders from arrows, and machicolations, or floor openings, through which missiles could be fired down on attackers.

baluster – upright post supporting the handrail on stairs.

bargeboard – wooden board protecting the eaves of a roof.

bay – a space of wall between any vertical element, such as an upright beam, pillar or a division into a window or door.

bay window – window projecting out from a flat wall, either canted if the sides are straight, or bowed if curved.

bolection mould – moulding concealing the join of vertical and horizontal surfaces, shaped like an S in cross-section.

Boulle – elaborate inlay work on the surface of furniture, customary in 17th and 18th-century French work.

bow – see bay window

canted – see bay window

cartouche – frame for a picture or statue, often oval and surrounded by a scroll.

caryatid – a column in the shape of a draped female figure.

casements – see sashes

chinoiserie – a style of advanced Rococo with Chinese motifs, often associated with Gothick.

coffering – a ceiling composed of beams enclosing sunken square or round panels.

collars – see roof timbers

corbel – a stone or wood projection in a wall that supports a beam, statue or window sill.

cornice – (1) a ledge or projecting upper part of a classical entablature. (2) Moulding at the top of a wall concealing the join with the ceiling.

cottage ornée – late-Georgian/Victorian picturesque cottage, usually with thatched roof and Gothic windows.

crenellation – see bailey

crocket – Gothic decorative device, usually a cusp or curling leaf, at regular intervals on outer edges of spires, pinnacles and gables

cruck – a simple structure of two, usually curved, trunks of wood formed into an inverted V which support the walls and roof of a medieval house.

curtain wall – in castle-building, a wall constructed between defensive projections such as bastions.

dentil – one of a series of small square blocks along the base of a cornice

dorter – a sleeping room or dormitory, especially in a college or monastery.

dressing – a general term for finishings; stone is dressed to either a smooth or ornamental surface.

enfilade – a line of rooms in sequence along one side of a house, usually with interconnecting doors.

entablature – a feature of classical architecture comprising everything above column height, formally composed of architrave, frieze and cornice.

flatwork – decorative plaster or woodwork in low relief.

frontispiece – a decorative bay above a doorway in a Tudor or Jacobean building, customarily composed of Renaissance motifs.

gable – the triangular end of a double-pitched roof, sometimes with stepped or scrolled (Dutch) sides.

garderobe – privy or lavatory, usually discharging into a ditch or moat outside a medieval house.

Great Chamber – see solar

grisaille – monochrome painting, usually a mural and in shades of grey.

grotesque – decorative wall motif of human figures, as found in Roman grottoes.

half-timbering – term for timber-framed house derived from the practice of splitting logs in half to provide beams.

hipped roof – a roof with a sloping end instead of an end gable.

Ho-Ho bird – chinoiserie motif associated with 18th-century Rococo style.

jetty or jettied floor – upper floor extended, or oversailed, beyond the lower one to give more space upstairs and to protect the lower walls from adverse weather. Jettying also uses the downward thrust of the upper walls to form a cantilever, preventing internal ceiling beams from bowing.

keep – see bailey

king post – see roof timbers

linenfold – a pattern on wall panels imitating folded linen.

louvre – a covered turret above a medieval hall that allowed smoke to escape.

machicolation – see bailey

mannerism – see Artisan Mannerist

mansard – a roof with two separate pitches of slope.

motte – see bailey

mullion – central divider of window, made of metal or stone.

oversail – see jetty

oriel – an upper window projecting from a wall, sometimes (incorrectly) used to indicate a tall medieval window lighting the dais end of the Great Hall.

Palladian – a style of classical architecture, formal and refined outside, often lavish inside, named after Italian architect, Andrea Palladio (1508–80). Moving spirit behind most English classical designers, especially Inigo Jones and, later, Lord Burlington, William Kent and the early Georgians.

parlour – see solar

piano nobile – the main ceremonial floor of a classical building, sitting on the basement or 'rustic' lower floor.

pier-glass – a wall mirror supported by a small table, bracket or console.

pietra dura – literally 'hard stone'; a decorative inlay using highly polished stones such as marble, jasper and porphyry

pilaster – a flat column projecting only slightly from a wall.

pointing – mortar or cement used to seal between bricks.

porte-cochère – a grand porch with a driveway through it, allowing passengers to alight from carriages under cover.

prodigy house – a large, ostentatious house of the Elizabethan/Jacobean period.

putti – unwinged sculptures of chubby boys found in Classical and Baroque decoration.

queen post – see roof timbers

quoins – dressed corner stones.

render – a covering of stucco, cement or limewash on the outside of a building.

Rococo – the final phase of Baroque style in the 18th century, typified by refined painted and plaster decoration, often asymmetrical and with figures.

roof timbers – a tie-beam runs horizontally across the roof space; a king post rises vertically from the tie beam to the apex of the roof; queen posts rise not to the apex but to subsidiary beams known as collars; wind-braces strengthen the roof rafters.

rustic – a name given in Palladian architecture to the lower floor or basement, beneath the piano nobile.

rustication – treatment of ashlar by deep-cutting joints so they look stronger or cruder.

sashes – windows opening by rising on sash ropes or cords, as opposed to casements which open on side hinges.

scagliola – composition of artificial stone that imitates appearance of grained marble.

screens passage – accessed from the main door of a medieval building and built into one end of a Great Hall to shield it from draughts. Door ors arches lead from the passage into the hall on one side and kitchens on other. Above is usually a minstrels' gallery.

Serlian – motifs derived from pattern books of the Italian Renaissance architect, Sebastiano Serlio (1475–1554).

sgraffito – plaster decoration scratched to reveal another colour beneath.

solar – the upstairs room at the family end of a medieval hall, originally above an undercroft or parlour. Originally accessed by ladder or spiral stairs, it was usually replaced by a Great Chamber in the Tudor era.

strapwork – strap or ribbon-like decorative scrolls in Elizabethan and Jacobean design.

stucco – plaster, usually protective, covering for brick, sometimes fashioned to look like stone.

studding – vertical timbers laid close to each other to strengthen the wall. Close-studding tends to indicate wealth.

tie-beam – see roof timbers

undercroft – a vaulted room or crypt beneath a building, partly or wholly underground

vault – a ceiling, usually of stone composed of arches.

Venetian window – Palladian window composed of three components, the centre one arched.

wind-braces – see roof timbers

Simon Jenkins' sources

The best guides to any house are the people who occupy it. They have felt its walls and sensed its seasons. They stand witness to its ghosts, real and imagined, and have thus become part of its history. As a substitute, guidebooks vary widely from the academic to the plain childish. The best are published by English Heritage, erudite and enjoyable. National Trust guidebooks are at last moving from the scholarly to the accessible, and the Trust's compendium *Guide*, by Lydia Greeves and Michael Trinick, is excellent.

My selection of a thousand properties derives from numerous sources. These include Hudson's *Historic Houses and Gardens*, supplemented by *Museums and Galleries* published by Tomorrow's Guides. The Historic Houses Association website is another invaluable source. Of recent house surveys, the best are John Julius Norwich's *Architecture of Southern England* (1985), John Martin Robinson's *Architecture of Northern England* (1986) and Hugh Montgomery-Massingberd's *Great Houses of England and Wales* (2000). Nigel Nicolson's *Great Houses of Britain* (1978) describes the most prominent. Their lists are not exhaustive and include houses not open to the public. Behind them stands Nikolaus Pevsner's massive 'Buildings of England' series, which deals with houses more generously (with plans) in the newer revised editions.

On English domestic architecture, the classics are hard to beat. They include Olive Cook's *The English House Through Seven Centuries* (1968), Alec Clifton-Taylor's *The Pattern of English Building* (1972), Hugh Braun's *Old English Houses* (1962), Sacheverell Sitwell's *British Architects and Craftsmen* (1964) and Plantagenet Somerset Fry's *Castles of Britain and Ireland* (1980).

On specific periods the best are Mark Girouard's *Robert Smythson and the English Country House* (1983), Giles Worsley's *Classical Architecture in England* (1995), Kerry Downes's *English Baroque Architecture* (1966) and Girouard's *The Victorian Country House* (1971). Joe Mordaunt Crook takes a lively look at the Victorian battle of the styles in *The Dilemma of Style* (1989). Jeremy Musson describes the manorial revival in *The English Manor House* (1999) and Gavin Stamp takes a wider look at the same period in *The English House 1860–1914* (1986). *Edwardian Architecture*, edited by Alastair Service (1975), brings the story into the 20th century and Clive Aslet's *The Last Country Houses* (1982) almost completes it.

On social history, Girouard's *Life in the English Country House* (1978) is incomparable. *Creating Paradise* (2000) by Richard Wilson and Alan Mackley sets the house in its economic context. So does Mordaunt Crook's *The Rise of the Nouveaux Riches* (1999) and David Cannadine's *The Decline and Fall of the British Aristocracy* (1990). Adrian Tinniswood offers a fascinating insight in his *History of Country House Visiting* (1989). The desperate post-war bid to save houses is described in Marcus Binney's *Our Vanishing Heritage* (1984) and John Cornforth's *The Country Houses of England 1948–1998* (1998). Peter Mandler covers the same period in his scholarly *The Fall and Rise of the Stately Home* (1997).

Biographies of architects are too legion to list but Howard Colvin's *Biographical Dictionary of British Architects* (1978) was my bible over disputed dates and attributions. Of a more personal character is James Lees-Milne's delightful account of the National Trust's early acquisitions in *People and Places* (1992). Houses in distress are visited in John Harris's *No Voice from the Hall* (1998). *Writers and their Houses* (1993) is a first-class collection of essays, edited by Kate Marsh.

I am indebted to the many architectural commentaries in *Country Life*, champion of the historic buildings cause for over a century. I do not believe I could have found a thousand houses for my list were it not for its progenitors, Edward Hudson and Christopher Hussey, and their many successors.

Contact details

Note: Readers are advised to check opening times before visiting, either via the websites and addresses below or in Hudson's Historic Houses & Gardens, the annual guide to castles, houses and heritage sites open to the public. Some houses included in the London East and London West sections have addresses in counties bordering London.

Apsley House – Hyde Park Corner, London W1J 7NT www.english-heritage.org.uk/apsleyhouse Tel 020 7499 5676 Open all year, Tue–Sun (also BHs Apr–Oct) 10am–5pm (to 4pm Nov–Mar)

Banqueting House – Whitehall, London SW1A 2ER www.banqueting-house.org.uk Tel 0870 751 5178 Open all year, Mon–Sat 10am–5pm

Basildon Park – Lower Basildon, Reading, Berkshire RG8 9NR www.nationaltrust.org.uk/basildonpark Tel 0118 984 3040 or 01494 755558 Open late Mar–Oct, Wed–Sun & BH Mon 12–5pm (grounds open at 11am)

Bear Wood – Bearwood College, Winnersh, Wokingham, Berkshire, RG41 5BG www.bearwoodcollege.berks.sch.uk Tel 0118 974 8300 Contact the school for visiting arrangements

Boston Manor – Boston Manor Road, Brentford, Middlesex, TW8 9JX www.hounslow.info/bostonmanor.htm Tel 0845 456 2800 Open Apr–late Oct, Sat, Sun & BHs 2.30–5pm

Buckingham Palace – London SW1A 1AA www.royalcollection.org.uk 020 7766 7300 The Queen's Gallery open all year, daily (though may be closed on certain days) 10am–5.30pm; The State Rooms open Aug–Sep, daily 9.45am–6pm; The Royal Mews open Mar–Oct, Sat–Thur 11am–4pm. Opening arrangements may be subject to change at short notice

Cabinet War Rooms – Clive Steps, King Charles Street, London SW1A 2AQ www.iwm.org.uk Tel 020 7930 6961 Open all year, daily 9.30am–6pm

Carlyle's House – 24 Cheyne Row, London SW3 5HL www.nationaltrust.org.uk 020 7352 7087 Open late Mar–late Oct, Wed–Sun & BH Mon 2–5pm (from 11am on Sat, Sun & BH Mon)

Charlton House – Charlton Park, Charlton Road, London SE7 8RE Tel 020 8856 3951 Open for group tours by arrangement only, and on some open days throughout the year

Chiswick: Chiswick House – Burlington Lane, London, W4 2RP www.english-heritage.org.uk/chiswickhouse Tel 020 8995 0508 Open Apr–Oct, Wed–Sun & BHs 10am–5pm; Nov–Mar for pre-booked tours only

Chiswick: Hogarth's House – Hogarth Lane, Great West Road, London, W4 2QN www.hounslow.info/hogarthshouse Tel 020 8994 6757 Open Feb–Dec, Tue–Fri (closed Good Fri) 1–5pm (to 4pm Nov–Mar); Sat, Sun & BH Mon 1–6pm (to 5pm Nov–Mar)

Clandon Park – West Clandon, Guildford, Surrey www.nationaltrust.org.uk/clandonpark Tel 01483 222482 Open late Mar–late Oct, Tue–Thur, Sun, BH Mon, Good Fri & Easter Sat 11am–5pm

Claremont – Claremont Fan Court School, Claremont Drive, Esher, Surrey, KT10 9LY www.claremont-school.co.uk Tel 01372 467841 Contact the school for viewing information. Also: Claremont Landscape Garden, Portsmouth Road, Esher, Surrey, KT10 9JG www.nationaltrust.org.uk/claremont Tel 01372 467806 Open all year, daily (closed Mon Jan–late Mar & Nov–late Dec) 10am–6pm (to 5pm Jan–late Mar & Nov–late Dec)

Dartmouth House – 37 Charles Street, London W1J 5ED www.esu.org.uk Tel 020 7529 1550 Contact for visiting arrangements

Dennis Severs House – 18 Folgate Street, London E1 6BX www.dennissevershouse.co.uk Tel 020 7247 4013 Open Mon evenings after dark for candlelit viewing (but not BHs); open first & third Sun of each month (2–5pm) and the Mon after these Suns (12–2pm)

Dickens' House – 48 Doughty Street, London WC1N 2LX www.dickensmuseum.com 020 7405 2127 Open all year, daily 10am–5pm (from 11am on Sun)

Down House – The Home of Charles Darwin, Down House, Luxted Road, Downe, Kent, BR6 7JT www.english-heritage.org.uk/downhouse Tel 01689 859119 Open early Feb–mid Dec, Wed–Sun (daily in mid Jul–late Aug) 10am–6pm (to 5pm mid Jul–late Aug & Oct, to 4pm Nov–mid Dec & early Feb–late Mar)

Eastbury Manor House – Eastbury Square, Barking, Essex, IG11 9SN www.nationaltrust.org.uk or www.barking-dagenham.gov.uk Tel 020 8724 1000 Open all year, Mon–Tue & 1st & 2nd Sat of the month 10am–4pm

Eltham Lodge – The Royal Greenwich & Blackheath Golf Club, Court Road, Eltham, London SE9 5AF www.rbgc.com Tel 020 8850 1795 Contact the golf club for access information

Eltham Palace – Court Yard, Eltham, London, SE9 5QE www.elthampalace.org.uk or www.english-heritage.co.uk/eltham Tel 020 8294 2548 Open early Feb–late Dec, Sun–Wed 10am–4pm (to 5pm Apr–Oct)

Englefield House – Contact Estate Office, Englefield Estate, Englefield Road, Theale, Reading, Berkshire, RG7 5DU www.englefieldestate.co.uk Tel 0118 930 2504 Gardens open all year, Mon (Mon–Thur in Apr–Oct) 10am–6pm; house open for group tours by prior arrangement

Eton College – Windsor, Berkshire, SL4 6DW www.etoncollege.com Tel 01753 671177 Open Mar–early Oct, contact the school for opening days and times

Farnham Castle – Farnham, Surrey, GU9 0AG www.farnhamcastle.com Tel 01252 721194 Open all year, Wed 2–4pm

Fenton House – Windmill Hill, London, NW3 6RT www.nationaltrust.org.uk Tel 020 7435 3471 Open early Mar–late Oct, Wed–Sun & BHs (Sat & Sun only early–late Mar) 2–5pm (from 11am at weekends)

Forty Hall – Forty Hill, Enfield, Middlesex, EN2 9HA www.enfield.gov.uk/fortyhall Tel 020 8363 8196 Open all year, Wed–Sun 11am–4pm

Freud's House – 20 Maresfield Gardens, London, NW3 5SX www.freud.org.uk Tel 020 7435 2002 Open all year, Wed–Sun 12–5pm

Fulham Palace – Bishop's Avenue, London, SW6 6EA www.fulhampalace.org Tel 020 7736 8140 Open all year, Mon–Tue 12–4pm, Sat 11am–2pm, and Sun 11.30am–3.30pm

Godalming: Red House – Frith Hill Road, Godalming, Surrey, GU7 2DZ Private house – can be partially viewed from public highway. (Photograph on page 168 taken from grounds of Charterhouse School.)

Great Fosters – Stroude Road, Egham, Surrey, TW20 9UR www.greatfosters.co.uk Tel 01784 433822 Now a hotel; gardens open all year

Greenwich: Flamsteed House, Queen's House and Royal Naval Hospital – National Maritime Museum, Park Row, Greenwich, London, SE10 9NF www.nmm.ac.uk Tel 020 8858 4422 Open all year, daily 10am–5pm (later in summer months)

Grim's Dyke Hotel – Old Redding, Harrow Weald, Harrow, Middlesex, HA3 6SH Tel 020 8385 3100

Guildford: Abbot's Hospital – The Hospital of the Blessed Trinity, High Street, Guildford, Surrey, GU1 3AJ www.abbotshospital.org Tel 01483 562670 Open all year, Mon–Sat for tours by prior arrangement

Guildford: Guildford House – 155 High Street, Guildford, Surrey, GU1 3AJ www.guildfordhouse.co.uk Tel 01483 444742 Open all year, Tue–Sat 10am–4.45pm

Gunnersbury Park – Pope's Lane, London, W3 8LQ Tel 020 8992 1612 Open all year, daily 1–5pm (to 4pm Nov–Mar)

Hall Place – Bourne Road, Bexley, Kent, DA5 1PQ www.hallplaceandgardens.com Tel 01322 526574 Open all year, daily (Tue–Sat only in Nov–Mar) 10am–5pm (from 11am on Sun & BHs, to 4.15pm in Nov–Mar)

Ham House – Ham, Richmond, Surrey, TW10 7RS www.nationaltrust.org.uk/hamhouse Tel 020 8940 1950 Open late Mar–late Oct, Sat–Wed 2–5pm; gardens open all year Sat–Wed 11am–6pm

Hampton Court Palace – Hampton Court Road, Hampton Court, Surrey, KT8 9AU www.hampton-court-palace.org.uk Tel 0870 752 7777 or 0870 751 5175 Open all year, daily 10am–6pm (to 4.30pm Nov–Feb)

Handel House – 25 Brook Street, London W1K 4HB www.handelhouse.org Tel 020 7495 1685 Open all year, Tue–Sun 10am–6pm (to 8pm on Thur & from 12pm on Sun)

Hatchlands Park – East Clandon, Guildford, Surrey www.nationaltrust.org.uk Tel 01483 222482 Open early Apr–late Oct, Tue–Thur, Sun & BH Mon (& Fri in Aug) 2–5.30pm

Home House – 20 Portman Square, London W1H 6LW
www.homehouse.co.uk Tel 020 7670 2000 Contact for visiting arrangements

Dr Johnson's House – 17 Gough Square, London EC4A 3DE
www.drjohnsonshouse.org Tel 020 7353 3745 Open all year, Mon–Sat
(closed BHs) 11am–5pm (to 5.30pm May–Sep)

Keats House – Keats Grove, London, NW3 2RR
www.cityoflondon.gov.uk/keats Tel 020 7435 2062 Open all year, Tue–Sun
1–5pm and also to visits by appointment Tue–Fri 10am–12pm

Nos. 1 & 2 Kensington Court – Milestone Hotel, 1 Kensington Court,
London W8 5DL www.hotel-at-kensington-gardens.co.uk Tel 020 7584 6454

Kensington Palace – London W8 4PX www.kensington-palace.org.uk
Tel 0870 751 5170 Open all year, daily 10am–6pm (to 5pm Nov–Feb)

Kenwood House – Hampstead Lane, London, NW3 7JR
www.english-heritage.org.uk/kenwoodhouse Tel 020 8348 1286
Open all year, daily 11am–5pm (to 4pm Nov–Mar)

Kew Palace – Kew Gardens, Kew, Richmond, Surrey, TW9 3AB
www.hrp.org.uk/kew Tel 0870 751 5179 Open late Mar–late Oct, Tue–Sun
10am–6pm

Lambeth Palace – Lambeth Palace Road, London SE1 7JU Tel 020 7898
1200 Open Feb–Nov (closed Aug) for tours on Thur (at 11am & 2pm) and
Fri (at 11am), although may be subject to alteration

Leighton House – 12 Holland Park Road, London W14 8LZ
www.rbkc.gov.uk/leightonhousemuseum Tel 020 7602 3316 Open all year,
Wed–Mon 11am–5.30pm

Linley Sambourne House – 18 Stafford Terrace, London W8 7BH
www.rbkc.gov.uk/linleysambournehouse Tel 020 7602 3316 (X 300) Mon–Fri
or 07976 060160 at weekends Open mid-Mar–mid-Dec, Sat & Sun for tours
starting 10am, last tour 3.30pm. Groups by arrangement at other times

Lord Chancellor's Residence – Palace of Westminster, St Margaret Street,
London SW1A 1AA Tel 020 7219 3000 Contact the Houses of Parliament
for access information

Loseley Park – Guildford, Surrey, GU3 1HS www.loseley-park.com
Tel 01483 304440 Open May–Sep, Tue–Sun (& BH Mon in May & Aug)
11am–5pm

Marble Hill House – Richmond Road, Twickenham, Middlesex, TW1 2NL
www.english-heritage.org.uk/marblehill Tel 020 8892 5115 Open Apr–Oct,
Sat 10am–2pm, Sun & BHs 11am–5pm and tours on Tue & Wed at 12pm &
3pm; Nov–Mar for pre-booked tours only

Nonsuch Mansion House – Nonsuch Park, Ewell Road, Cheam, Surrey,
SM3 8AL House situated within public park; museum open Apr–Sep, every
2nd & 4th Sun in the month & BH Mons 2–5pm; contact Hon Sec of Friends of
Nonsuch Mansion House (020 8642 2845) for further viewing information

Orleans House Octagon – Orleans House Gallery, Riverside, Twickenham,
Middlesex, TW1 3DJ www.richmond.gov.uk Tel 020 8831 6000
Open all year, Tue–Sun & BH 1–5.30pm (from 2pm on Sun & BH, closing at
4.30pm Oct–Mar)

Osterley Park – Jersey Road, Isleworth, Middlesex, TW7 4RB
www.nationaltrust.org.uk/osterley Tel 020 8232 5050 Open early Mar–late
Oct, Wed–Sun (Sat & Sun only early–late Mar) 1–4.30pm; grounds open all
year, daily 9am–7.30pm or dusk if earlier

Pitzhanger Manor – Walpole Park, Mattock Lane, London, W5 5EQ
www.ealing.gov.uk/pmgalleryandhouse Tel 020 8567 1227 Open all year,
Tue–Sat 1–5pm (from 11am on Sat)

Polesden Lacey – Great Bookham, Nr Dorking, Surrey, RH5 6BD
www.nationaltrust.org.uk/polesdenlacey Tel 01372 452048
Open mid-Apr–late Oct, Wed–Sun (& BH Mons from Easter) 11am–5pm;
grounds open all year, daily 11am–5pm or dusk if earlier

Rainham Hall – The Broadway, Rainham, Havering, Essex, RM13 9YN
www.nationaltrust.org.uk Tel 020 7799 4552/3 Open Apr–Oct, Sat & BH
Mon 2–5pm

Ranger's House – Chesterfield Walk, Blackheath, London SE10 8QX
www.english-heritage.org.uk/rangershouse Tel 020 8853 0035 Open
Apr–Sep, Sun–Wed 10am–5pm; also open Oct–Mar for prebooked tours only

Red House – Red House Lane, Bexleyheath, Kent, DA6 8JF
www.nationaltrust.org.uk Tel 01494 755588 Open Mar–Dec, Wed–Sun &
BH Mon 11am–4.15pm for prebooked tours only

Royal Holloway College – Egham Hill, Egham, Surrey, TW20 0EX
www.rhul.ac.uk 01784 434455 Contact the college for visiting arrangements

Royal Hospital Chelsea – Royal Hospital Road, London SW3 4SR
www.chelsea-pensioners.co.uk Tel 020 7881 5200 Open all year, daily
(closed BHs & Sun in Oct–Mar) 10am–12pm & 2–4pm

St Barnabas – The House of St Barnabas in Soho, 1 Greek Street, London
W1D 4NQ www.houseofstbarnabas.org.uk Tel 020 7437 1894
Contact for visiting arrangements

St John's Gate – Museum of the Order of St John, St John's Gate, London
EC1M 4DA www.sja.org.uk/museum Tel 020 7324 4070 Open all year,
Mon–Sat (closed BHs & Sat on BH weekends) 10am–5pm (to 4pm on Sat)

Soane Museum – Sir John Soane's Museum, 13 Lincoln's Inn Fields, London
WC2A 3BP www.soane.org Tel 020 7405 2107 Open all year, Tue–Sat
(closed BHs) 10am–5pm (6–9pm on first Tue of the month)

Southside House – 3 Woodhayes Road, London, SW19 4RJ
www.southsidehouse.com Tel 020 8946 7643 Open Easter Sun to early Oct,
Wed, Sat, Sun & BH Mon for tours at 2pm, 3pm & 4pm

Spencer House – 27 St James's Place, London SW1A 1NR
www.spencerhouse.co.uk Tel 020 7524 1958 Open all year (except Jan &
Aug), Sun 10.30am–5.45pm

Strawberry Hill – St Mary's, Strawberry Hill, Waldegrave Road,
Twickenham, Middlesex, TW1 4SX Tel 020 8240 4224/4044 Open early
May–late Sep, Sun 2–3.30pm

Sutton House – 2 & 4 Homerton High Street, Hackney, London E9 6JQ
www.nationaltrust.org.uk Tel 020 8986 2264 Open early Feb–late Dec,
Thur–Sun & BH Mon 12.30–4.30pm

Syon House – Syon Park, Brentford, Middlesex, TW8 8JF
www.syonpark.co.uk Tel 020 8560 0882 Open late Mar–late Oct, Wed,
Thur, Sun & BHs 11am–5pm

Titsey Place – Oxted, Surrey, RH8 0SD www.titsey.org Tel 01273 407017
Open mid-May–late Sep, Wed & Sun (plus some BHs in summer) 1–5pm

Tower of London – London EC3N 4AB www.tower-of-london.org.uk
Tel 0870 756 6060 or 0870 751 5177 Open all year, daily 9am–6pm
(10am–5pm on Sun & Mon). Closes 1 hour earlier, Nov–Feb

Valence House – Becontree Avenue, Dagenham, Essex, RM8 3HT
www.lbbd.gov.uk Tel 020 8270 6865 Open all year, Mon–Sat
10am–4.30pm (to 4pm on Sat)

Vestry House – Vestry Road, Walthamstow, London, E17 9NH
www.lbwf.gov.uk 020 8509 1917 Open all year, Mon–Sat 10am–1pm &
2–5.30pm (to 5pm on Sat)

Welford Park – Newbury, Berkshire, RG20 8HU Tel 01488 608203/608691
Open early Jun–late Jul, Mon–Sat 11am–5pm

Wesley's House – 47 City Road, London EC1Y 1AU
www.wesleyschapel.org.uk 020 7253 2262 Open all year, daily (closed BHs,
except Good Fri) 10am–4pm (12–1.45pm on Sun)

Westminster Abbey: Little Cloister – Dean's Yard, London SW1P 3PA
www.westminster-abbey.org Tel 020 7654 4900 Open all year; Abbey
open Mon–Sat 9.30am–3.45pm (to 6pm on Wed & 1.45pm on Sat);
main cloisters open daily 8am–6pm; college garden open Tue–Thur
10am–6pm (to 4pm Oct–Mar)

Whitehall – 1 Malden Road, Cheam, Surrey, SM3 8QD
www.sutton.gov.uk/leisure/heritage/whitehall.htm Tel 020 8643 1236
Open all year, Wed–Sun & BH Mon 2–5pm (from 10am on Sat)

William Morris House – Lloyd Park, Forest Road, Walthamstow, London,
E17 4PP Tel 020 8537 3782 Open all year, Tue–Sat and 1st Sun in each
month, 10am–1pm & 2–5pm

2 Willow Road – London, NW3 1TH www.nationaltrust.org.uk
Tel 020 7435 6166 Open early Apr–late Oct, Thur–Sat 12–5pm (5–9pm
on first Thur in each month); also open early–late Mar & early–late Nov, Sat
12–5pm

Windsor: The Castle & Queen Mary's Dolls' House – Contact
Information Office, Buckingham Palace, London SW1A 1AA
www.royalcollection.org.uk Tel 020 7766 7304 or 01753 831118 (infoline)
Open all year, daily (except 14 Apr & 19 Jun) 9.45am–5.15pm (to 4.15pm
Nov–Mar). Opening arrangements may be subject to change at short notice

Index

Main entries for houses are in **bold**

Discover Britain's Historic Houses: London, Berkshire & Surrey

Reader's Digest Project Team
Series editor Christine Noble
Art editor Jane McKenna
Picture researcher Christine Hinze
Caption writer/copy editor Caroline Smith
Proofreader Ron Pankhurst
Indexer Marie Lorimer
Product production manager Claudette Bramble
Production controller Katherine Bunn

Reader's Digest General Books
Editorial director Julian Browne
Art director Anne-Marie Bulat
Managing editor Alastair Holmes
Picture resource manager Sarah Stewart-Richardson
Pre-press account manager Sandra Fuller, Penelope Grose

Colour origination Colour Systems Limited, London
Printed and bound in Europe by Arvato, Iberia

We are committed to both the quality of our products and the service we provide to our customers. We value your comments, so please feel free to contact us on **08705 113366** or via our web site at **www.readersdigest.co.uk**

If you have any comments or suggestions about the content of our books, you can contact us at: **gbeditorial@readersdigest.co.uk**

Published by The Reader's Digest Association Limited, 11 Westferry Circus, Canary Wharf, London E14 4HE

www.readersdigest.co.uk

This book was designed, edited and produced by The Reader's Digest Association Limited based on material from *England's Thousand Best Houses* by Simon Jenkins, first published by Allen Lane, the Penguin Press, a publishing division of Penguin Books Ltd.

Concept code UK0149/L/S
Book code 634-005 UP0000-1
ISBN 978 0 276 44257 5
Oracle code 356600005H.00.24